motion◆motion
KINETIC ART

motion ◂▸ motion
KINETIC ART

Jim Jenkins & Dave Quick

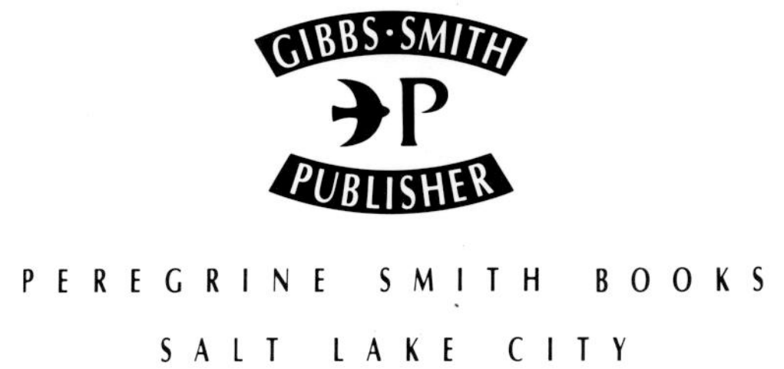

PEREGRINE SMITH BOOKS
SALT LAKE CITY

This is a Peregrine Smith Book, published by Gibbs Smith, Publisher. P. O. Box 667, Layton, Utah 84041

Design by Kathleen Timmerman

Printed and bound in Korea by Sung In Printing Company

Library of Congress Cataloging-in-Publication Data
Jenkins, Jim, 1955-
Motion motion kinetic art / by Jim Jenkins and Dave Quick
p. cm.
ISBN 0-87905-185-X
1. Kinetic sculpture, American. 2. Sculpture, Modern – 20th century – United States.
3. Regionalism in art. I. Quick, Dave, 1950- . II. Title.
NB212.5.K54J46 1989
709'.73.dc20 89-8496
CIP

Acknowledgements:
The Authors would like to thank all the artists and their galleries for their generous cooperation in granting interviews and providing photographs, and for their overall support of this book. In particular, a special thanks to Alice Aycock, Jonathan Borofsky, and Fletcher Benton for their time and interest as well. Also, we would like to extend our gratitude to our galleries (Koslow Gallery and Thinking Eye Gallery, both of Los Angeles) for their continued support throughout this entire project.

Dedications:
To Terri
Jim Jenkins
To Randi, Alexander, and Ian
Dave Quick

Contents

Introduction

FOR TWENTY YEARS, SCULPTURE INCORPORATING real time and movement has been regarded as an orphan of contemporary art. The Kinetic Art movement of the sixties is perhaps a classic example of the old adage, "the light that burns twice as bright burns half as long." Critics then and now tend to dismiss kinetic artwork as a novelty art form – a passing fancy.

However, the presixties pioneers of kinetics are not dismissed with such ease. Most notably, the investigations of Duchamp, Tinguely, and Calder in the early to mid-twentieth century were greeted with the same awe and respect as the other new approaches which collectively have molded the twentieth century into the most visually challenging century of all. In fact, it can be said that efforts of these three men led to the Kinetic Movement of the sixties. So what happened? How did the hallowed "art machine" have its plug pulled for a generation?

Falling Off the Bandwagon

IN THE WORLD OF FASHION, THE MOMENT A CERTAIN look is regarded as being "in" it is already "out." The minute popularity becomes recognized, mystique dies – the very idea Marshall McLuhan was talking about when speaking of the "cool" versus the "hot" image. It is human nature to be attracted to something that cannot be completely explained – curiosity breeds value in the mind of the observer. If one can equate art movements with the world of fashion, bandwagons have long been a part of twentieth century art history. The art bandwagon can best be defined as the efforts of the populace to cash in on the headway gained by a few visionaries. Unfortunately, this "bandwagonning" often dilutes and trivializes the inspired, original contribution by lessening the impact and aesthetic integrity of the initial form.

Such was the case with the Kinetic Movement of the sixties. Once setting sculpture in motion became popular, the seriousness of this element of art was lost and replaced by a battalion of mechanical, "look what I can make move" projects that detoured further and further away from the intent of visual expression. Critics were quick to identify the absence of content in these works, and the entire art form of kinetics was routinely panned.

Corporate Kiss of Death

CERTAINLY NOT ALL KINETIC SCULPTURE SPAWNED in the sixties could be so easily dismissed. The corporate-sponsored work of Experiments in Art and Technology (E.A.T.) were truly remarkable, though short-lived. New York's E.A.T. combined the technical prowess of state-of-the-art scientists with the poetic visual aptitude of artists, and a host of marvelous works resulted. Such works included a piece entitled *Nine Evenings,* staged in the Armory of the 69th Regiment in New York City in 1966, as well as in the fog-shrouded Pepsi Pavilion at the 1970 World's Fair in Osaka. These and other works have yet to be equaled. Corporate support rallied to contribute to such noble collaborations, and a small group of artists and engineers benefited. The results, though impressive, were at the same time intimidating to the isolated kinetic artist whose resources were not so abundant. Many such artists drifted back to more traditional forms of art, leaving the corporations to the kinetic art form until the next trendy investment opportunity arrived.

These factors, coupled with the inherent concern of collectors over regular maintenance of kinetic works, caused the lights to dim on the Kinetic Movement.

Benton, Aycock, and Borofsky

THE POSTSIXTIES KINETIC ART DROUGHT IS NOT without notable exceptions. Three major artists whose individual directions have incorporated motion into their works are Fletcher Benton, Alice Aycock, and Jonathan Borofsky. Their interest in motion represents a major sampling of kinetics among established artists working within the last twenty years.

San Francisco-based artist Fletcher Benton personally witnessed the rise and fall of the Kinetic Movement. He abandoned figurative painting in 1964 in search of a new format. He began to investigate the potential of geometry in his art. The resulting works featured solid color, the alphabet, and, as a means to activate the surface, motion. Benton's investigation of movement coincided with the relocation to Berkeley of Peter Selz from New York's Museum of Modern Art. Selz brought with him the plans for a major exhibition entitled "Directions in Kinetic Sculpture." The exhibition, which primarily featured European artists, showed the work of only three Americans: Charles Mattox, George Rickey, and Fletcher Benton. The resulting notoriety brought Benton into the international spotlight.

For the next ten years, Benton's work evolved through a number of different approaches – from light pieces that dealt with the Doppler Effect, to the application of transparent lacquer on acrylic sheeting. One example of Benton's style is a piece entitled *Rock and Roll.* In this work, a cylinder is rolled back and forth by the tilting track, creating different patterns within the cylinder. As the cylinder rolls past the center of the track, a blue light flashes within a rectangular base.

By 1974, Benton's interest in motion as an aesthetic dimension began to wane. He realized that he had made a drastic jump from a two-dimensional to a four-dimensional approach, skipping three-dimensional art altogether. At this same time, Benton also realized that the inherent maintenance and delicate shipping procedures of kinetic work proved to be too much of a distraction from the enjoyment of producing the work. He abandoned motion, pursuing his same geometric concepts in a series of monolithic steel works, which he claims still investigate the fourth dimension through the implied motion of tension and balance.

In contrast to Benton, the incorporation of motion into the monumental installations of New York artist

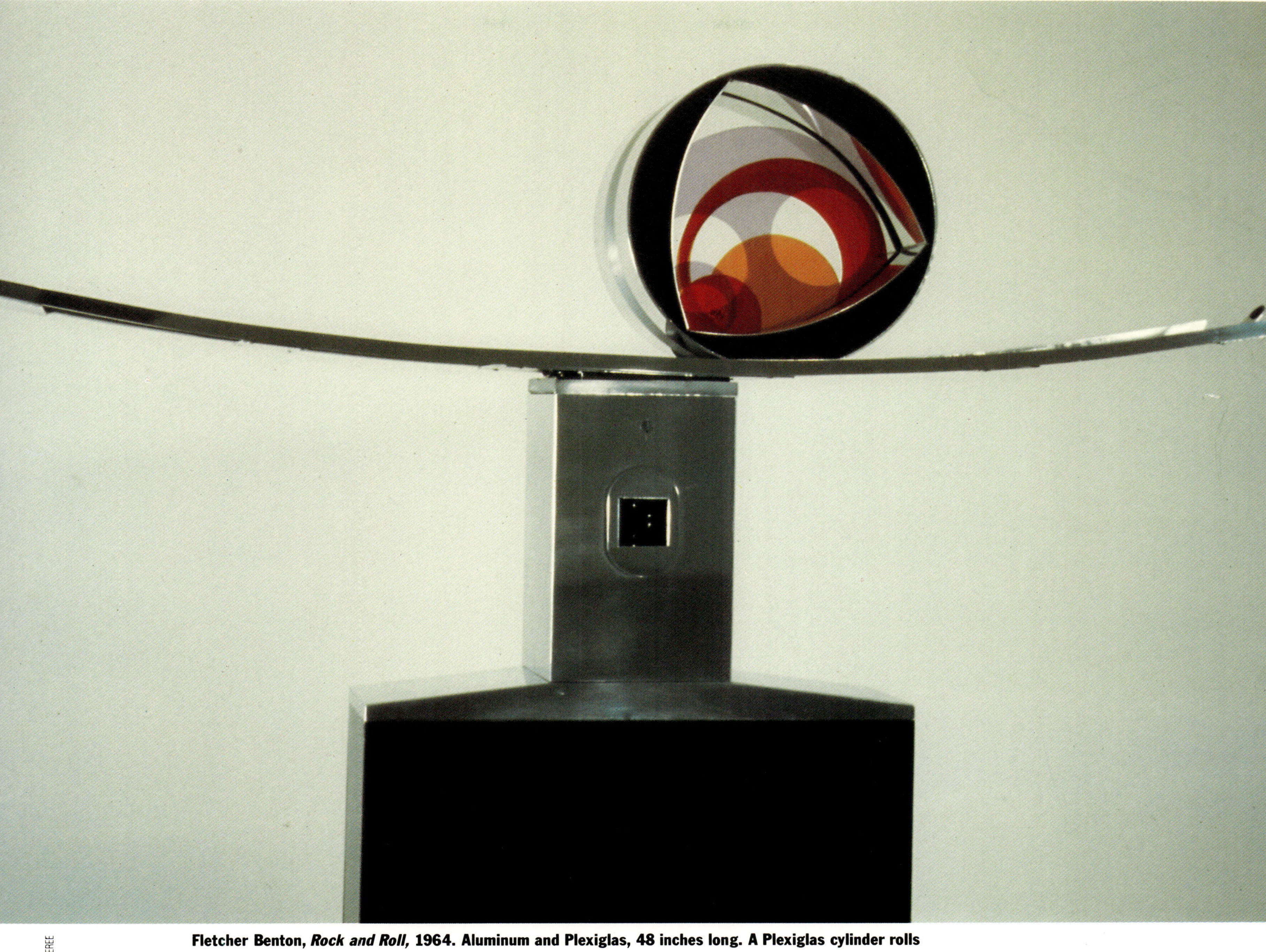

PHOTO BY LEE FARTHEREE

Fletcher Benton, *Rock and Roll,* 1964. Aluminum and Plexiglas, 48 inches long. A Plexiglas cylinder rolls back and forth along the tilting arm, creating multicolored patterns within the cylinder.

Alice Aycock has been much smoother. Working from an interest in building structures, Aycock used architectural history as a muse. Throughout the 1970s her sculptures were primarily constructed of wood and explored a varied but limited range of forms. As the decade began winding down, so too did Aycock's interest in the primitive look of her work. In an effort to facilitate the exploration of new, more curvaceous forms, she began expanding her materials to include metal, glass, and neon. Her earlier wooden works had frequently used the wheel and other circular forms, giving an industrial, mechanical feel to the work. Physically activating the works became a logical extension of this mode of expression.

Aycock's most prolific single series is her well-known blade machines. The trademark that conceptually connects her works is the repetitive use of a revolving scythe-type blade. In keeping with Aycock's fascination with historical iconography, designs for the blade pieces were based on fifteenth-and sixteenth-century alchemical drawings about creation. The use of the mechanized blade allowed her to deal with the inherent presence of violence. A fine line developed for Aycock as she searched for a compatible balance between motion and its relationship to the sculpture as a whole. Sometimes, if the movement was too visually powerful, the piece would not even be turned on. As the series matured, the blade works took on a smaller format – the motion became more subtle, tamed. In the mideighties, Aycock drifted away from motion, concentrating on static architecture from the same fifteenth- and sixteenth-century alchemical designs.

Jonathan Borofsky attributes his interest in motion all the back to the crib when the doodads of Fischer-Price mobiles successfully quelled the discomforts of his earliest childhood. He states:

> *Humor seems to be associated with moving art because of the whimsical chord it seems to strike in us. And moving works are definitely closer to whimsy than to tragedy. These pieces usually enliven one's imagination in a way that makes you smile rather than frown. I guess it goes back to childhood. We like to see movement. We count on watching movement every night on television. In New York City in the summer, people hang out in the windows to watch the activity in the streets. Possibly because it counteracts the movement in our minds.*

This innate need to see movement is what first led Borofsky to bring his own artwork to life in 1978. Having painted his now infamous *Hammering Men,* he sought to execute them three dimensionally. The

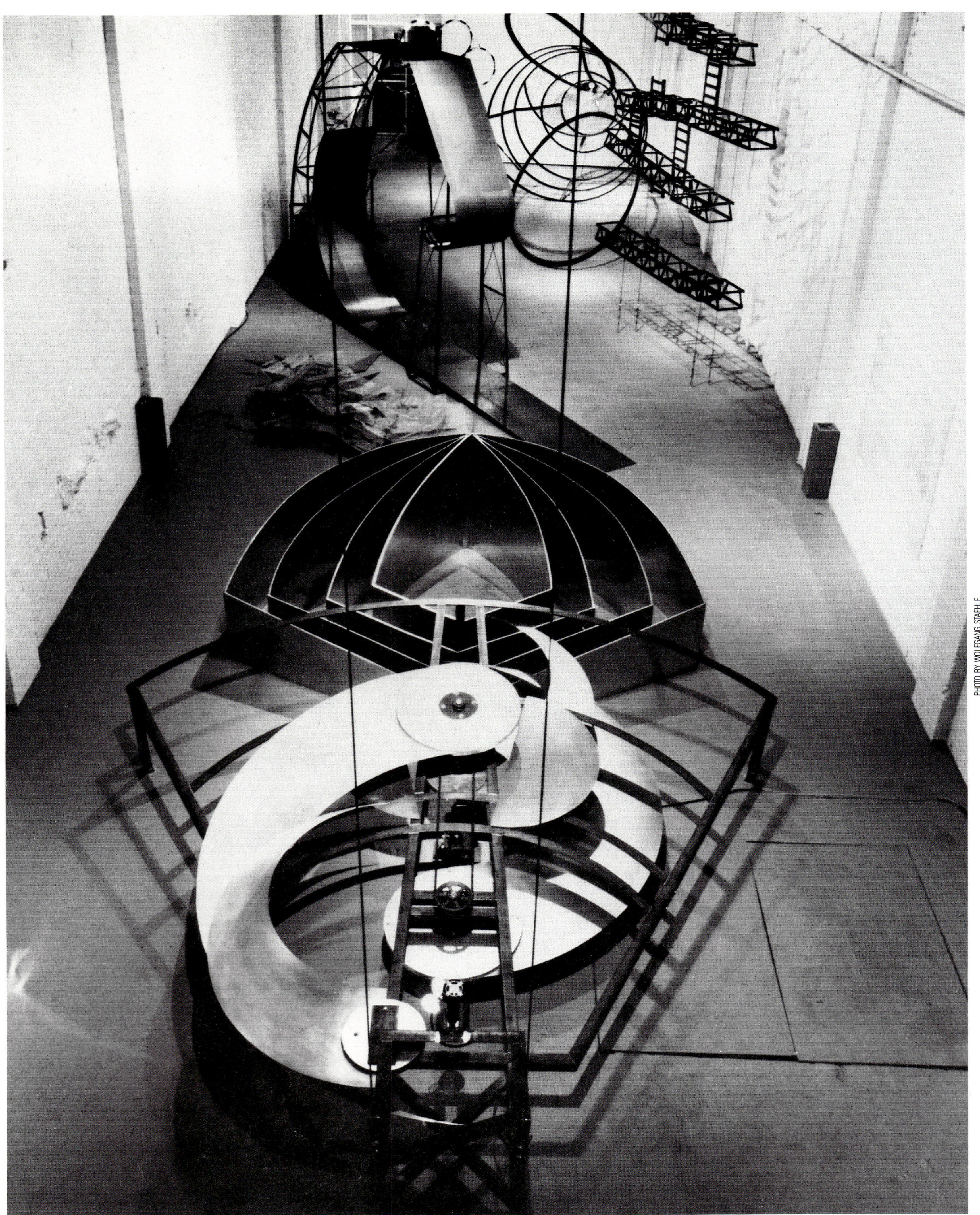

PHOTO BY WOLFGANG STAEHLE

Alice Aycock, *The Thousand and One Nights in the Mansion of Bliss,* 1983. Steel, galvanized sheet metal, Plexiglas, blinking lights, steel mesh, and motorized parts. Shapes for the revolving metal blades in Aycock's works are based on fifteenth- and sixteenth-century alchemy drawings about creation.

decision to animate the hammering arm soon followed. The visual impact of this towering figure continually wielding a club hammer met Borofsky's expectations. Having added the element of motion to his already vast repertoire of techniques, he developed a characteristically distinctive style of gallery installations. In 1983, the *Hammering Men* were joined by the *Chattering Men* series. These life-size, simplistically designed figures feature a movable metallic jaw, visibly activated by a motor positioned in the cranial region. A speaker inside the figure emits the endless passage of the words "chatter, chatter, chatter." The cant of the meditation owes homage to the artist's interest in Zen. Also, a visual connection is drawn between the visible motor/brain and the mouth.

As Benton and Aycock sought to avoid the issue of whimsy in their motion works, through the use of formalism and violence respectively, Borofsky actively pursues the reference and slyly caters to it.

PHOTO BY TORD LUND, COURTESY STATENS KONSTMUSEER – THE NATIONAL SWEDISH ART MUSEUMS

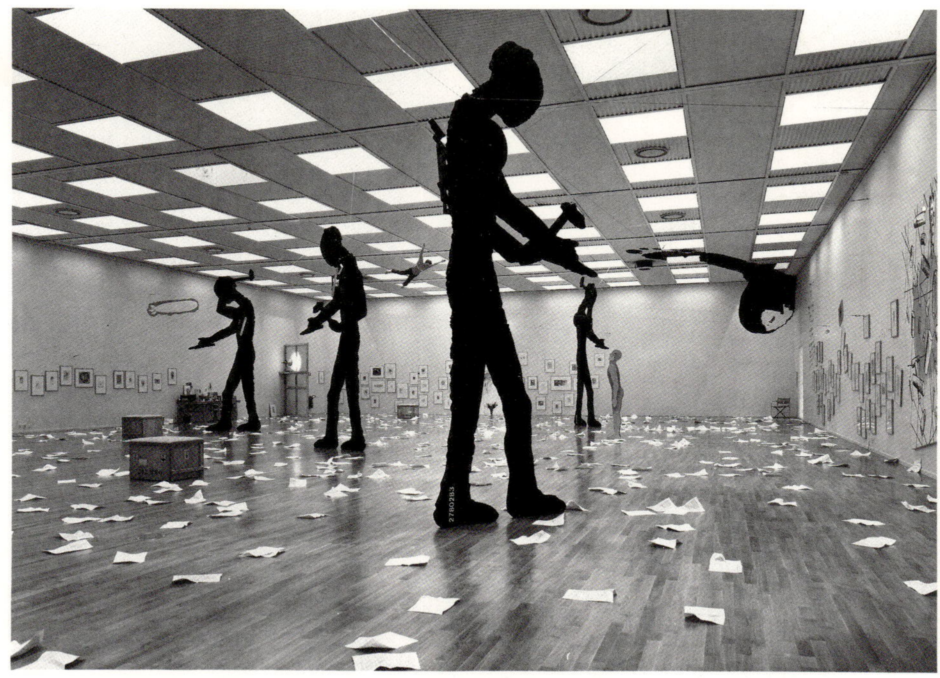

Jonathan Borofsky's, *Hammering Men* installation, 1984, based on a series of earlier paintings by the artist.

The Kinetic Art Movement Revival

ALONG WITH THE KINETIC OUTPUT OF SUCH LUMINARIES as Aycock and Borofsky, the eighties have witnessed a resurgence of kinetic art exhibitions.

On the East Coast, three regional exhibitions of note were all organized solely, or in part, by New York City curator Tom Finkelpearl. The first, "Mechanisms," was at the P.S. 1 Gallery in 1984. The second in 1986 was at the Clocktower and was entitled "Engaging Objects: The Participatory Art of Mirrors, Mechanisms, and Shelters." The following year, Finkelpearl collaborated with major supporter and collector of motion works, David Bermant, to organize an exhibit entitled "P.U.L.S.E (People Using Light, Sound, Energy)." The P.U.L.S.E. exhibit took place at one of Leo Castelli's galleries in the heart of New York's fashionable Soho district and received substantial media attention.

In the Midwest, Chicago's N.A.M.E. Gallery presented a 1982 exhibition entitled "Desiring Machines" which featured Chicago-area artists. In 1987, one of the few national efforts to unite kinetic artists was organized by the Kohler Arts Center of Sheboygan, Wisconsin. The exhibition, "Eccentric Machines," was curated by Joanne Cubbs and included work of twenty artists from various regions of the United States.

On the West Coast, two important regional exhibitions are worthy of mention. In 1985 a show called "Loco-Motion" was curated by Linda Lyons at California State University at Los Angeles. A second exhibition, "New Visions," was set at the 1986 Los Angeles Fairplex at Pomona in the cavernous halls of the Fine Arts Pavilion. An enormous effort organized by Kim and Dave Svenson, the exhibition displayed not only kinetic works, but neon and laser art as well.

One mainstay of the Los Angeles arts community since its inaugural opening in 1982 is the Museum of Neon Art. Director/Founder Lili Lakich proudly acknowledges the museum to be unique in its mission to exhibit and preserve works of neon, kinetic, and electric art. No other institution in the country, perhaps the world, maintains the dedication to solely exhibit these forms of art.

With early movement giants such as Duchamp, Calder, and Tinguely, and postseventies majors such as Benton, Aycock, and Borofsky, kinetic sculpture clearly has an ample historical base. The seduction of art by science in the sixties – the well-financed collaborations backed by corporate America – are history. Thankfully departed is the "gee-whiz" art machine fad that trivialized the sculpture-motion relationship. Man has now walked on the moon, the space shuttle has exploded, and art has reclaimed from science its integrity as a right-brain pursuit even when working with science and industry. An unmistakable conclusion drawn from this book's survey is that artists working with motion are doing so as artists, not aspirant engineers or pseudoscientists. Chicago sculptor Gary Justis notes that "...in the battle between art and science, art will win because it has no boundaries."

The last twenty years have yielded a group of dedicated artists who have continued to keep art's legitimate investigation of the fourth dimension alive. Some of the artists surveyed incorporate movement in all their work, while others incorporate movement only occasionally. All, however, perceive motion as a valid language of art.

PHOTO BY BEN BLACKWELL, COURTESY PAULA COOPER GALLERY

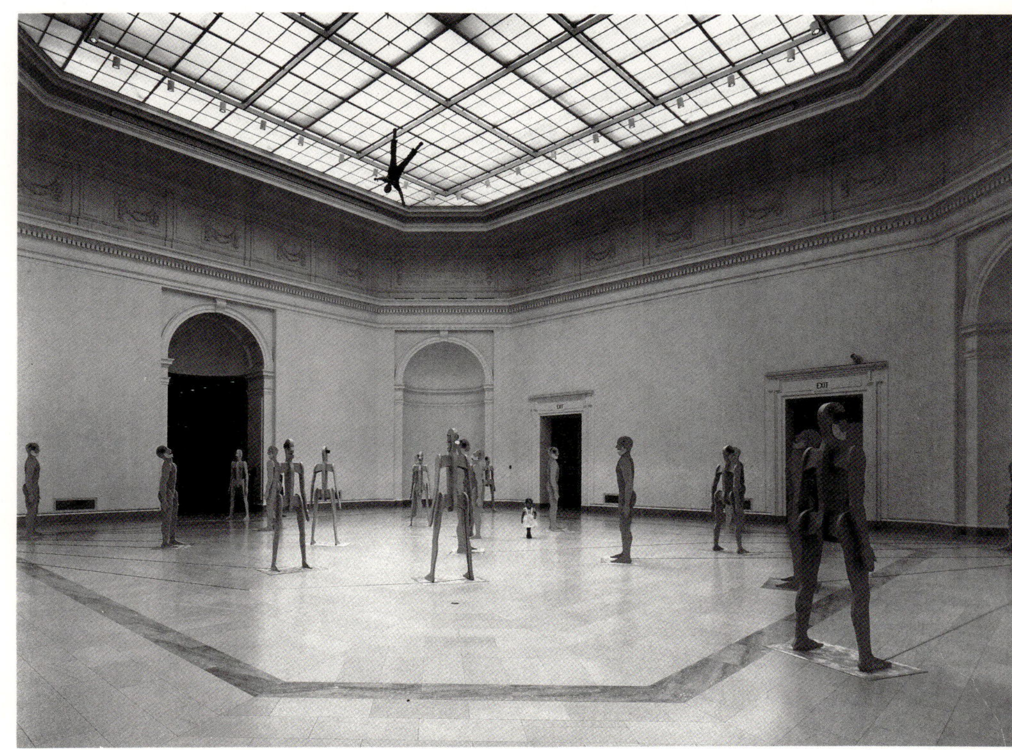

Jonathan Borofsky, *20 Chattering Men*, 1984. Aluminum, wood primer, electric motors, speakers. These life-sized figures are fitted with small speakers from which continually emanate the words "chatter, chatter, chatter."

Lewis Alquist

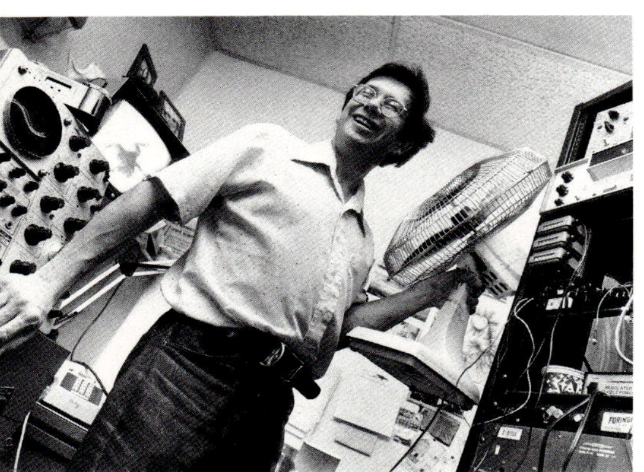

PHOTO BY JOHN GIPE

FROM THE JUNK STORES OF CHICAGO to the shipyards of San Francisco, Phoenix-based artist Lewis Alquist has little trouble collecting inspiration, and materials, for his unique brand of electrically activated sculptures. Alquist's characteristically larger than life-size works feature a wide range of common objects that vary from fans to beds to automobile windshields.

Alquist states, "Real objects make the work accessible. I enjoy the tradition of the objects utilized in the work. They become our contemporary mythology."

Confessing an influence that lies embedded with the "ready-made" mentality of the Dadaists, Alquist started to explore the parallels between machinery and eroticism early in his career. Tracing this idea specifically back to Duchamp and Picabia, he continues to recognize the age-old symbols of masculine and feminine that resurface again and again. However, Alquist's intent goes deeper still.

Sharing Alice Aycock's fascination with the mystery of the laws of nature, Alquist's works become active demonstrators for the presence of the forces of nature within our own existence. Using eroticism as a subliminal formal element for the composition of the work, it is both the hidden and visually evident forces that are harnessed and primarily displayed within the parameters of each piece.

In 1983, Alquist constructed a piece entitled *States of Matter Undergoing Habitual Rotation.* In this work, two identical dwarfed metal bed frames are spun at different velocities. The slower one holds a glass liner partially filled with a light-colored opaque liquid. As this bed revolves, centrifugal force causes the liquid to rise up the sides of the liner, creating a parabolic-shaped depression in the center. Thus, what easily read as liquid at first, has now taken on the shape of a gravity-defying solid object. The second bed, which has been left unaltered, is spun at a much greater speed, making its form airy and indistinguishable. As a result, the solid appearance of the metal bed now has the look of some sort of blurry gas. Besides being a simple demonstration comparing the states of solid, liquid, and gas, Alquist's utilization of the beds as the vehicle initiates a disturbing scenario. Such an initiative becomes commonplace in Alquist's work as it thrives on teasing the fine line that separates light comedy and harsh reality.

Such was the case with a work executed several years later entitled, *Hot Lunch.* This work consisted of a long, graphite-coated table set upon the top of an inverted, charred-metal coffin stand. Atop the table rests one red Fiesta dinnerware plate. Embedded in the ends of the table are Geiger sensors. The table is motorized to slowly flop back and forth as a see-

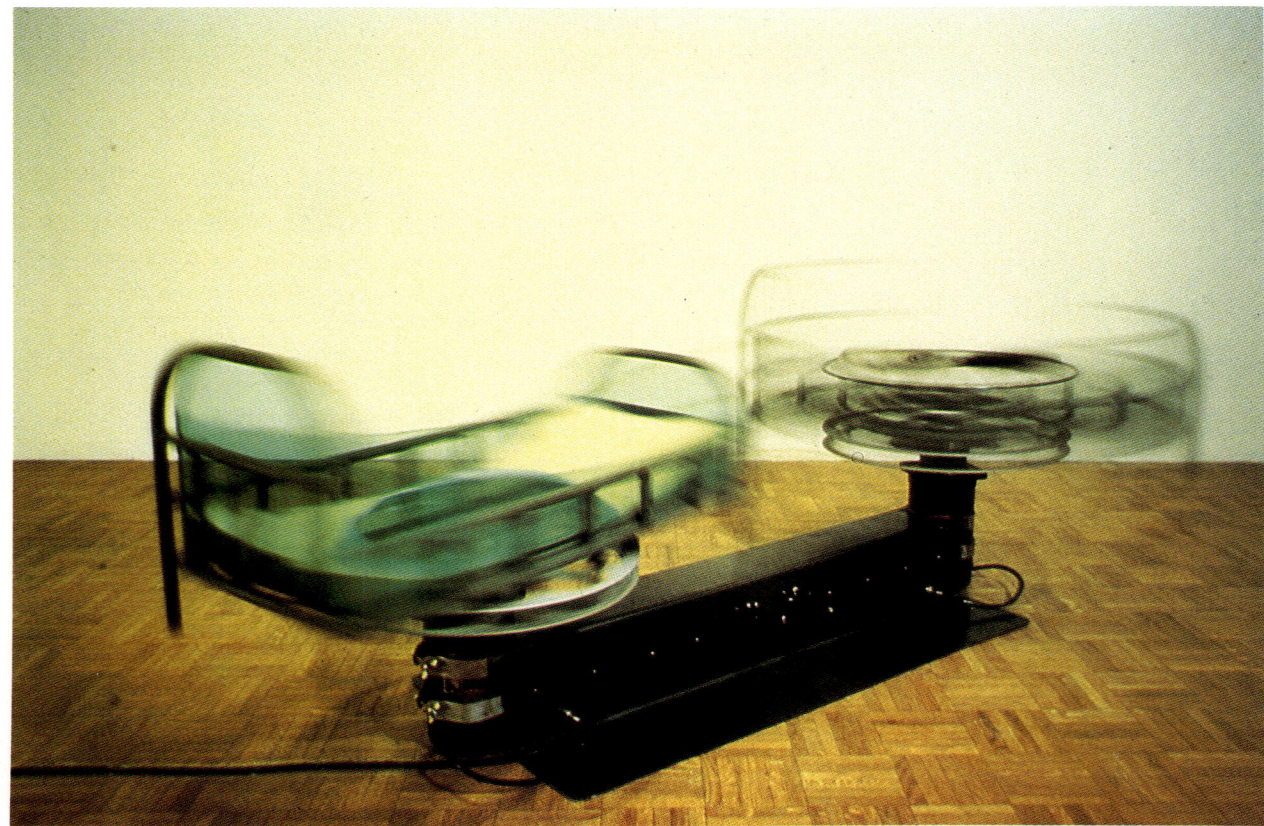

Lewis Alquist, *States of Matter Undergoing Habitual Rotation,* 1983. Steel bed frames, glass, motors, milk substitute. 24x30x72 inches. Two small bed frames spin at different speeds. One is filled with a liquid which, as the bed spins, forms a solid-looking parabolic shape.

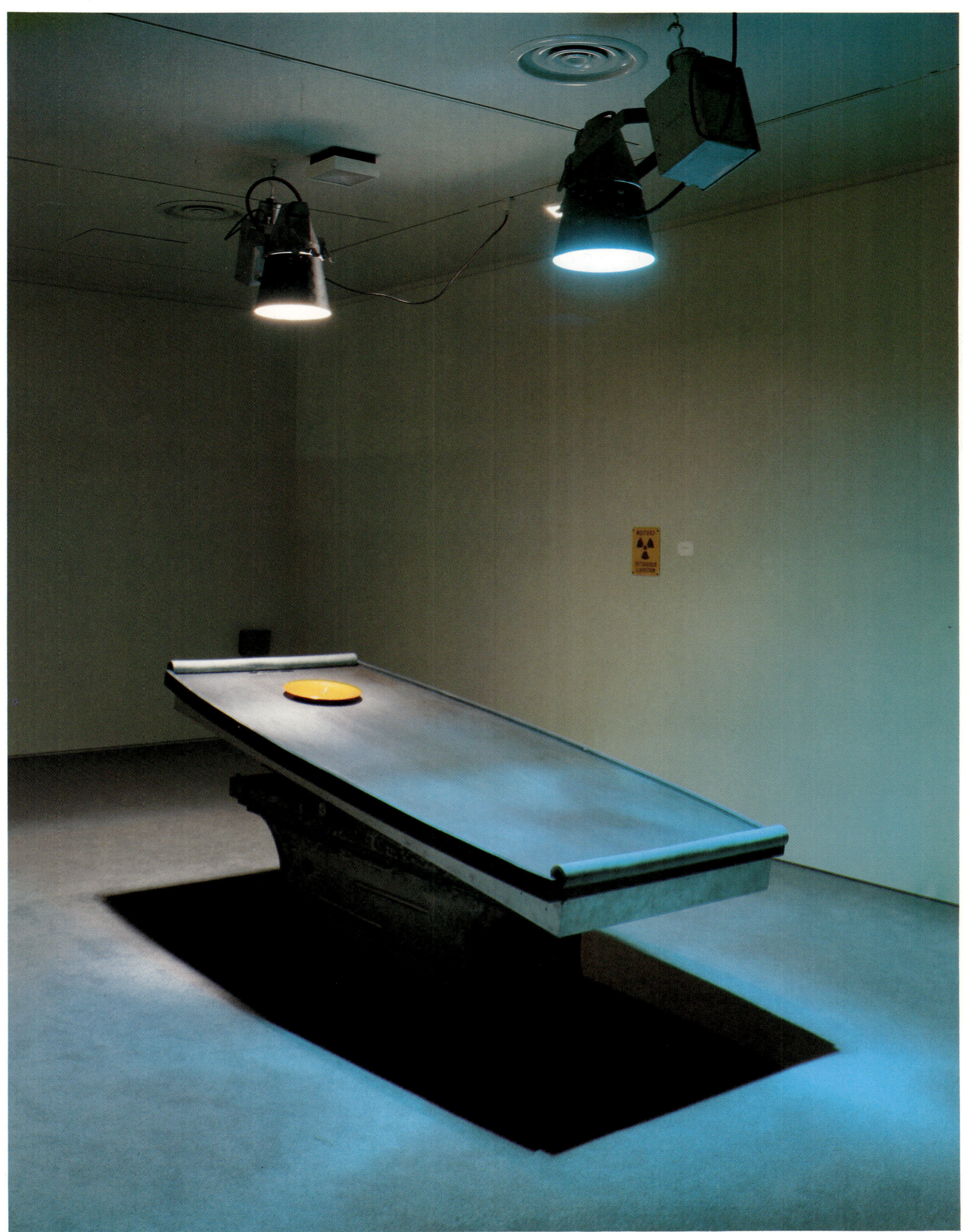

Lewis Alquist, *Hot Lunch*, 1987. An uranium-containing Fiesta dinnerware plate is slid back and forth across a teetering table. Situated on each end of the table are Geiger sensors that crackle loudly when the plate slides above them.

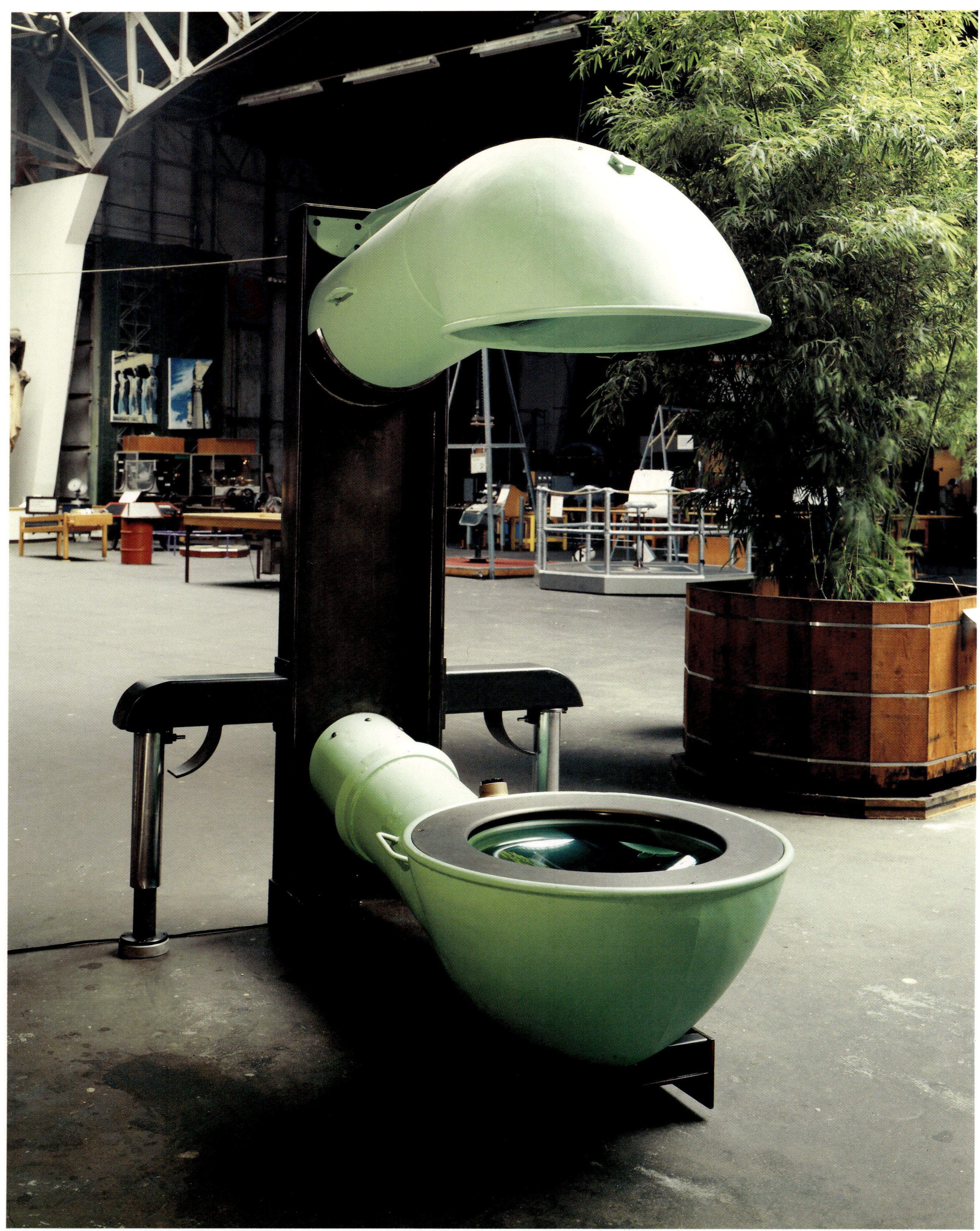

Lewis Alquist, *Fickle Oracle,* 1986. Steel, glass, electronic components, mercury. 96x84x62 inches. A spinning dish of mercury forms a parabolic liquid mirror in the lower scoop. The upper unit houses a flat tilted mirror. By means of a knob the viewer can change the spinning speed and, therefore, the focal length of the mercury mirror and the interplay of images between the two reflecting units.

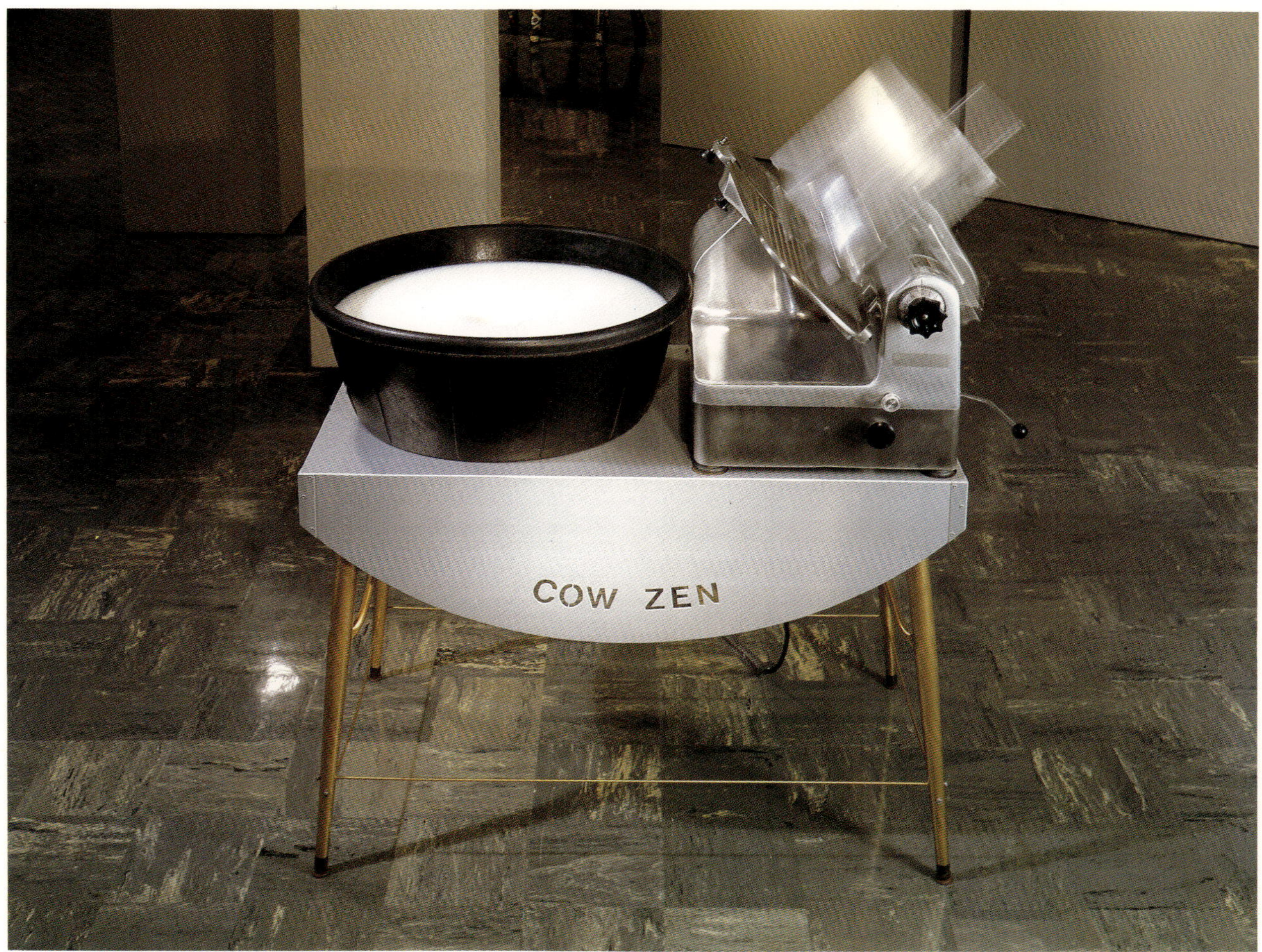

Lewis Alquist, *Cow Zen,* 1987.
A milk substitute is inwardly stirred to create an eddy while an adjacent meat slicer continually attempts to slice nothing.

saw, causing the plate to slide from one end of the table to the other. Through research, Alquist discovered that the red glaze used on Fiestaware, as well as other midcentury ceramics, contained uranium. Thus, as the plate slides down to the end of the table, alighting atop the Geiger sensor, speakers broadcast the consequent crackling sound throughout the gallery. Clearly, the symbolism of the two-sided table exchanging, or rather denying, the potent plate strikes a rather unnerving international chord.

A 1986 grant from the National Endowment of the Arts helped to fund both *Hot Lunch* and a second project dealing with the same radiation motif. In this piece, entitled *Sleeping Mutation,* Alquist pays homage to French sculptor Constantin Brancusi by placing an emu egg on a similar Fiestaware plate, which in turn rests atop a Geiger counter. The shape of the egg curiously echoes that of the head in Brancusi's *Sleeping Muse.* The Geiger counter again crackles from the uranium-embedded glaze of the plate. Alquist comments that the work is also inspired by the fact that a developing embryo is the most sensitive to radioactivity.

"I view art as a series of mutations, some of which work and some that don't."

Probably one of Alquist's most ambitious projects to date came about upon receiving a sculpture commission, in 1985, from the Exploratorium in San Francisco. Functioning as a hands-on museum, the Exploratorium features a variety of exhibits that invite young and old alike to experience the marriage of art and science. Mindful of the visual impact of the opaque liquid in the *States of Matter* spinning bed, Alquist was intrigued with the potential of a liquid mirror while playing with a small amount of mercury in a Petri dish. In an effort to heighten the visual sensation of this phenomena, Alquist procured 180 pounds of mercury that were to become the focal point of the resulting work entitled *Fickle Oracle.*

A variable-speed spinning dish filled with the mercury is located inside the receiving end of a salvaged marine air scoop. The spinning action of the dish causes the mercury to curve into a parabola and form a variable-focus liquid mirror. A second scoop is positioned parallel overhead and holds a flat mirror tilted at an angle. When viewers approach the pool they see two images: one of themselves looking through and down, and another of the spectators behind the sculpture looking through the cylindrical shaft of the upper scoop. By turning a knob on the lower scoop, the viewer causes the mercury pool to change speed and, proportionally, its focal length. Slowly increasing the speed shows an undulating panorama of reflected images that appears to be getting smaller. Decreasing the speed makes objects reflected overhead appear to get larger and close in from above.

Although towering eight feet in the air, *Fickle Oracle* has a disarming quality about it. The word "oracle" in the title refers to a shrine consecrated to a prophetic god. In *Fickle Oracle* viewers may approach this "well of mirror" and manipulate their own visual destiny by turning the knob that controls the amount of recognition/distortion in the resulting image. As viewers straddle the lower scoop and twist the control now positioned between their legs, the recurring themes of dominance/passiveness and eroticism continue to afford them power over the physicalities of the work.

Commenting on the mentally interactive nature of his work, Alquist states, "Historically, an evolution has taken place that has moved from the kinetic artists of the sixties that just showed off the technology, in retrospect appearing immature, to the state now where it's more into the human response."

Mineko Grimmer

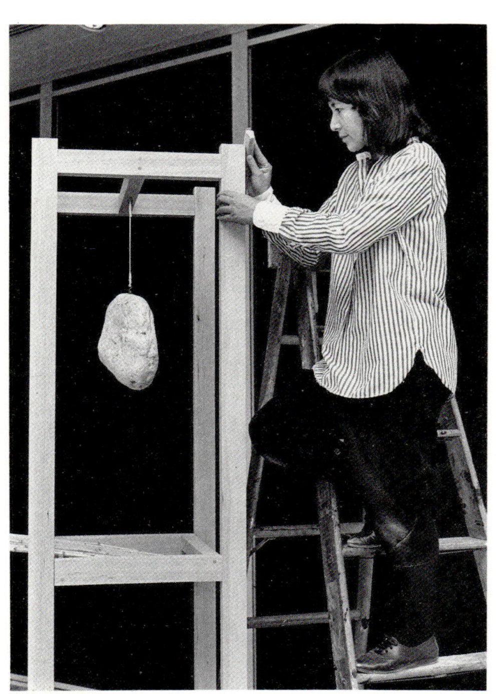

PHOTO BY STEVEN RUBIN

IN REVIEWING MINEKO GRIMMER'S *Ice Stone Wood Bamboo* show at San Francisco's Bruce Velick Gallery (April–May 1988), one distinguished Bay Area art critic declared that the artist has "solved" the media of installation – that she represents the apex of installation as an art form after which all other artists will be merely runners-up!

Perhaps overstated in this one instance, only slightly less euphoric superlative reviews have accompanied Grimmer's exhibitions from Los Angeles to New York, suggesting an inordinate poignancy to her work. Since the early eighties, Grimmer has been investigating an installation format that has remained fairly linear in development – a format that incorporates motion. A representative example is Grimmer's *Symposium,* a "talking" bamboo sculpture installed at New York's Whitney Museum (January 1988) and Los Angeles's Koplin Gallery (April 1988). *Symposium* contains four eight-foot-tall wooden towers surrounding a square pool. Each tower holds two assortments of horizontal bamboo poles that extend out over the pool. Centered over the bamboo is a pyramid-shaped block of pebbles frozen in ice. As the ice melts over the course of the day, the pebbles fall through the bamboo and into the growing pool of water. As the pebbles fall, they strike the bamboo, "talking" on the descent with a final "plunk" into the water.

Variations of the theme include *Seeking the Philosopher's Stone* where the pebbles strike taut wire, in effect creating a percussion string instrument played randomly. In *Spiral Tower,* the pebbles are suspended above two twisting wooden rectangles with horizontal, bamboo pole dividers. Other Grimmer installations have utilized dowel matrices. Her studio is replete with maquettes of future installations which again vary the theme of stone's journey from ice through sound and return to earth.

Mineko Grimmer was born and grew up in Japan where she studied commercial art. She moved to the United States with her American husband in 1980, and enrolled in the Otis/Parsons Art School in Los Angeles. As her biography would suggest, her art represents a hybrid of Eastern sensibilities and Western conceptualism. Her constructions owe homage to traditional Japanese carpentry – they are built of unpainted pine, sectioned and joined with dowels instead of nails. The form composition of her installations suggests a hybrid of traditional Japanese architectural lines (strongly rectilinear) and Western minimalism.

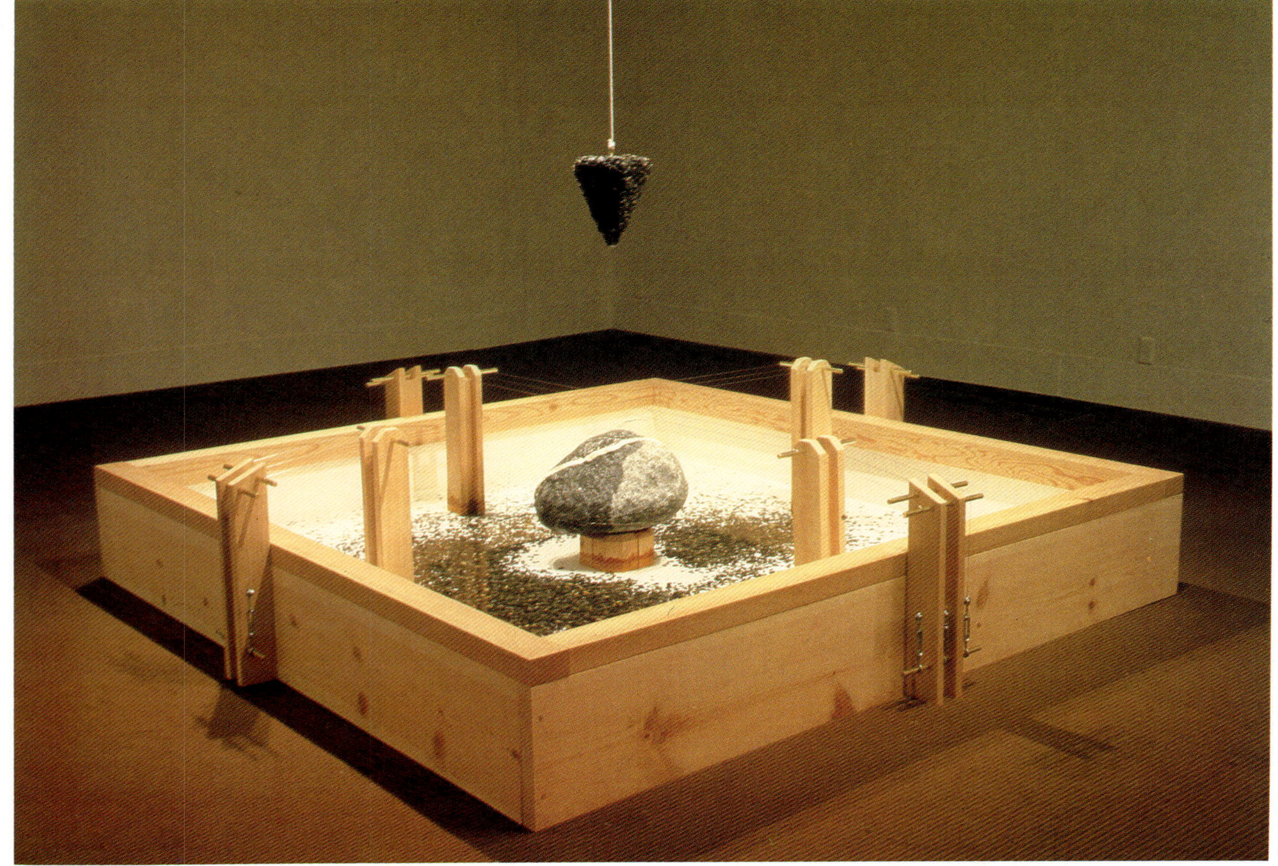

PHOTO BY GREY CRAWFORD

Mineko Grimmer, *Seeking the Philosopher's Stone,* 1985. Pebbles falling from the melting ice block strike taut wire, creating a random "playing" of the percussion string.

PHOTO BY STEVEN RUBEN

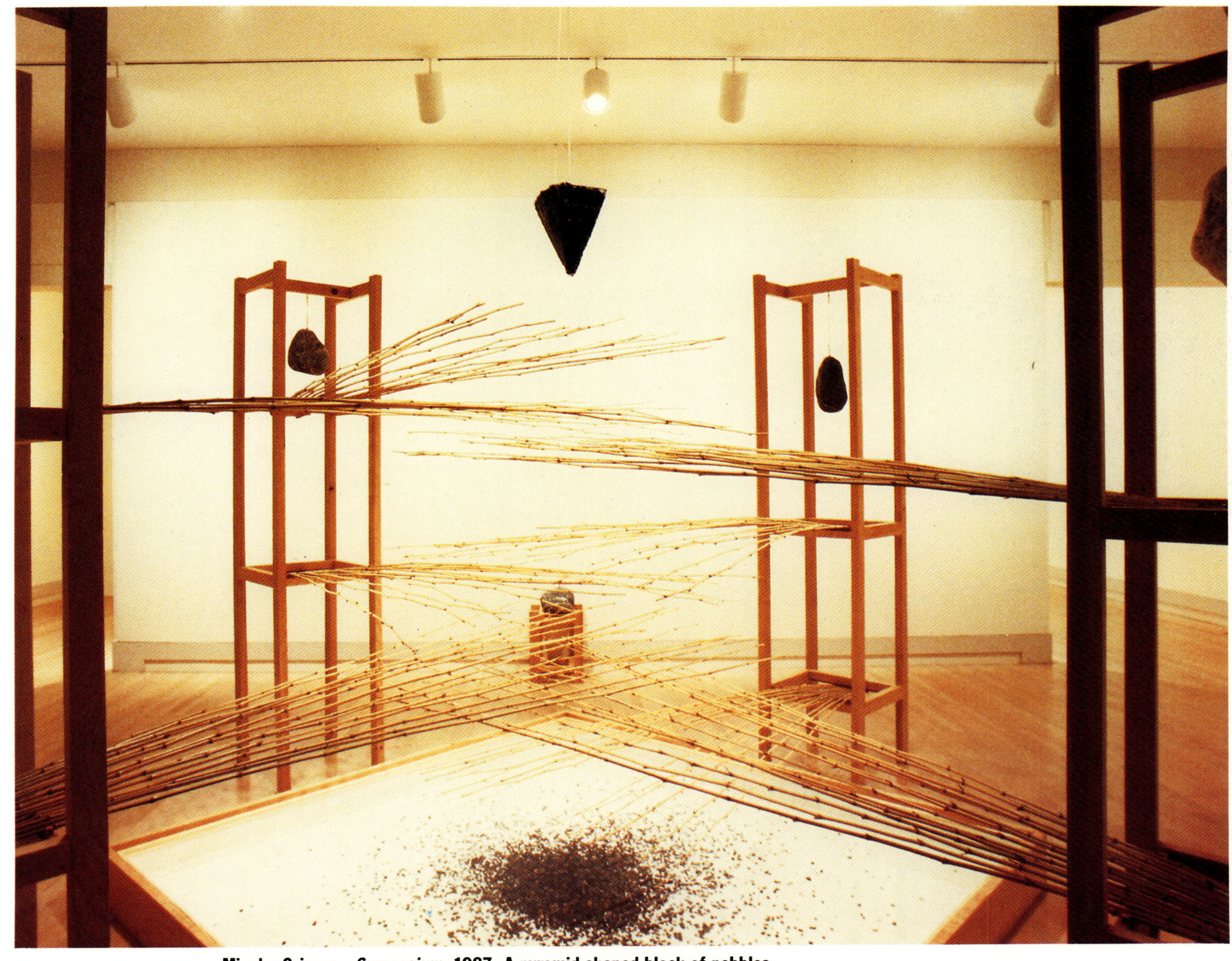

Mineko Grimmer, *Symposium,* 1987. A pyramid-shaped block of pebbles frozen into ice melts over the course of the day, causing the pebbles to fall through the bamboo poles into the shallow pool of water.

Her choice of materials is similarly minimalist in flavor – wood, stone, ice, bamboo – materials respectful of Shintoist reverence of nature. The meditative character of Grimmer's installations recall Japan's Buddhism.

Grimmer's early U.S. investigations were in collaboration with composer Carl Stone. One of her earliest pebble-fall installations was a dual performance with Stone entitled *Audible Sculpture – Musical Composition.* From there evolved the thematic constants found in *Symposium* nearly a decade later. The motion of her work provides sound. It also provides journey. It creates a "controlled randomness" within the structured environment of the installation. The falling pebbles create a pattern in the tradition of fallen leaf patterns of Shinto shrines. The inevitability of ice melting and pebbles falling is reaffirmation of the forces of heat and gravity at work. There is within the tight economy of Grimmer's work whole cycles of renewal – giant metaphors for a human condition where the only constant is the motion of change.

Grimmer's installations address the issue of control versus randomness and entropy. We cannot control change, we can only strive to create an inner philosophical framework in which we accommodate change. While Grimmer may not have "solved" the challenge of the installation as an art form, it would be difficult to identify a more provocative format. Grimmer works in the rarefied air of cross-cultural universal truths.

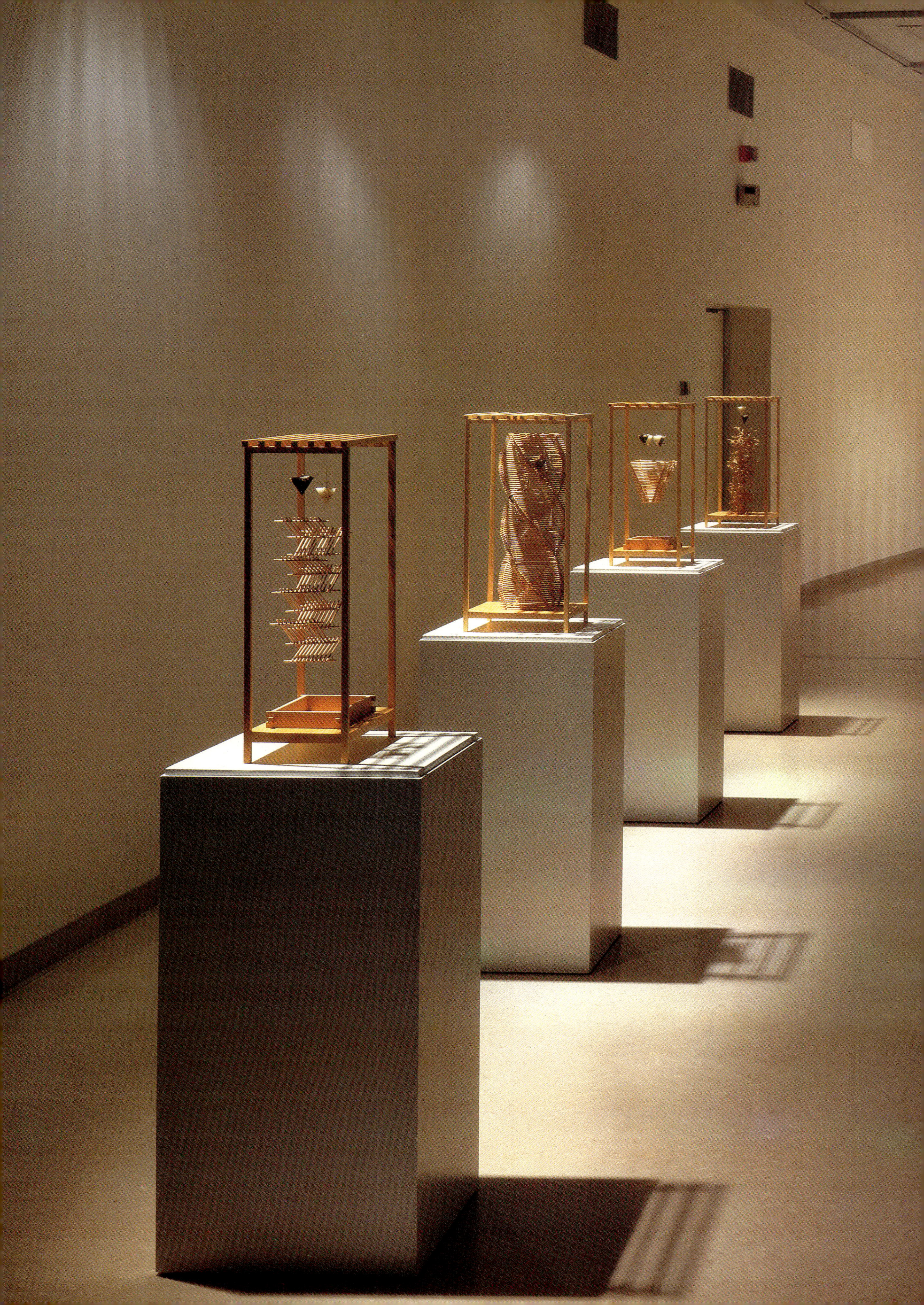

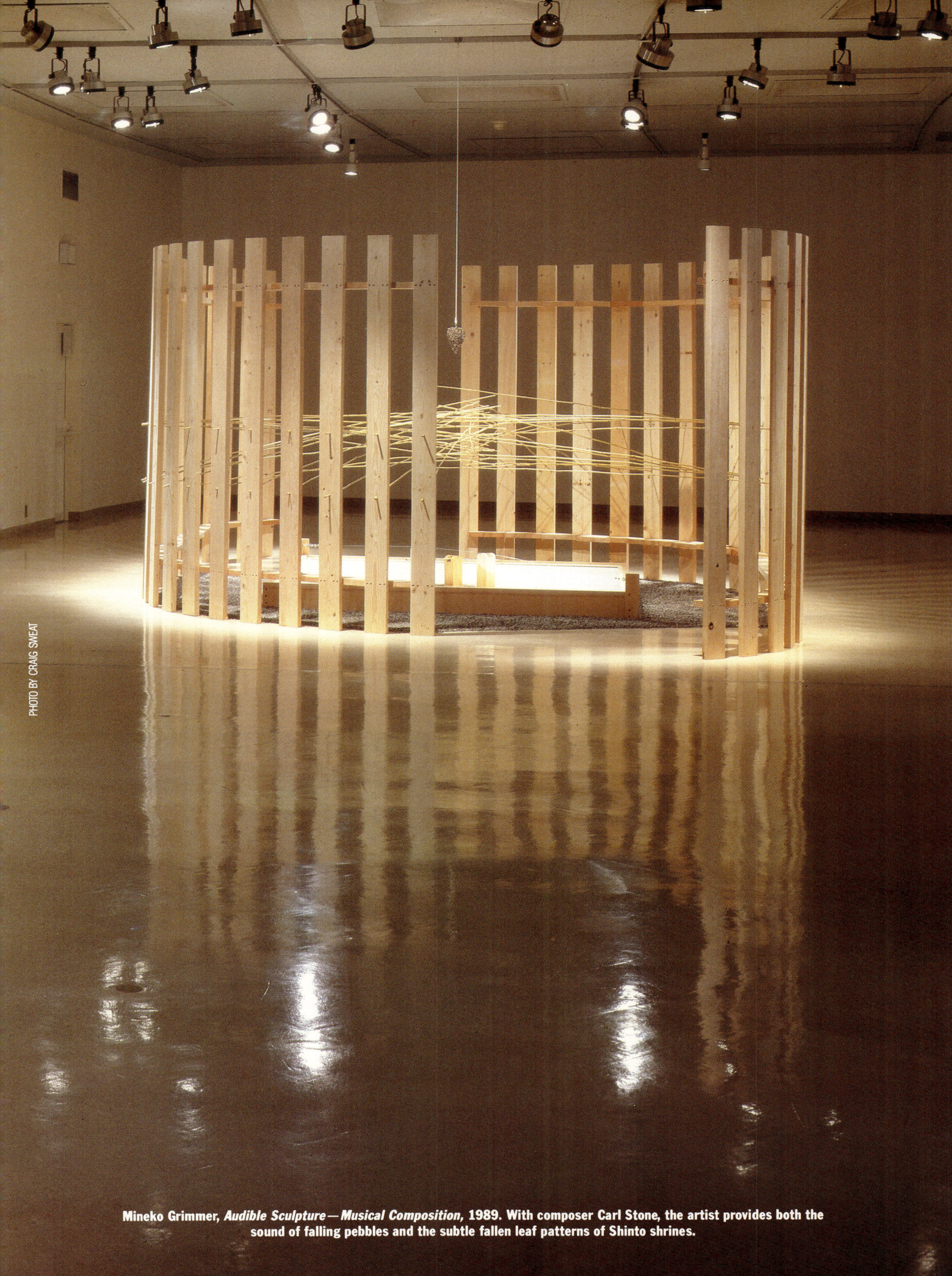

PHOTO BY CRAIG SWEAT

Mineko Grimmer, *Audible Sculpture—Musical Composition,* 1989. With composer Carl Stone, the artist provides both the sound of falling pebbles and the subtle fallen leaf patterns of Shinto shrines.

Jim Jenkins

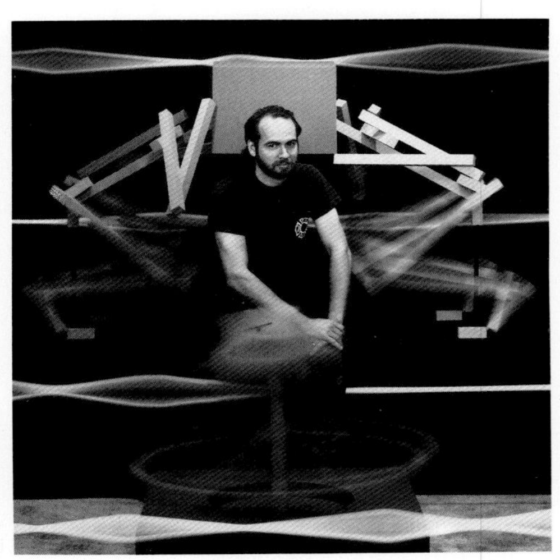

FOR JIM JENKINS THE ISSUE HAS never been whether to use motion in sculpture, but how to best conduct a continuing investigation of motion as a multifaceted element of visual language. In Jenkins's body of work, motion becomes metaphor for relationship, time awareness, and force beyond human control.

Jenkins's earliest works utilized motion as both time marker and animator of relationships. A good example is *Fiehl* in which a bronze female faceplate is raised and lowered and knocks back and forth with a male face counterpart, suggesting the motion of a tactile encounter. In *Fiehl* the motion is intermittent – broken by seemingly random long spells of silence. The piece then reactivates suddenly and unannounced. The intermittent silence is as important as the motion once it occurs. Motion serves to define time. Jenkins is establishing that interpersonal exchange exists only in opposition to the silence of loneliness. Movement becomes the sculptor's metaphor for human interaction. All time perception is measured by motion against nonmovement.

Sa Sa Cha Cha is a major gallery installation – an extravaganza of primitive forms that activate in sequence to pound bamboo poles upon the floor. When all members are hammering away the sound is deafening. An extension of earlier small-scale investigations, Jenkins is redefining "tribalism" as a shared activity relationship, not merely residence in the same village.

As the World Turns spoofs the greatest tribal glue of America – television. A major installation, this work puts in spinning motion over the viewer's head a life-size TV, an easy chair, and a channel changer that collectively assume the motion of the Sun, Earth, and Moon. With the TV as the center of the universe, this work becomes a visual extension of the intrusion of TV's moving pictures into the mindlessness of the soap opera-watching life-style. *Video Rodeo* treats the moving pictures of TV as components of a larger moving assemblage, as baby boomer Jenkins pays snide homage to a childhood of TV westerns.

Jim Jenkins, *Sa Sa Cha Cha,* 1983. Each figure is 6 feet high and is motorized to tap its bamboo poles on the floor in a variety of different sequences and rhythms. The 16 figures are separated into two groups of 8 each and face each other from opposing sides of the gallery. This arrangement allows for members from one group to tap out a "message" of sorts, then stop to wait for the other group to respond.

The son of a retired USAF engine mechanic, Jenkins assigns his preoccupation with machines and motion to major childhood influences derived during the "fantasy fifties" – a time when faith in science and machine was at an all-time high (the atomic bomb won the war!). One influence was the movie *Babes in Toyland* where madcap inventor Ed Wynn had a magic toy-making machine. Another was the movie *Flubber* where Fred McMurray had a rainmaking machine. Young Jenkins was so inspired by the later that he rushed home to build his own rainmaking machine. For Jenkins, machines exist not as objects, but as process, consistent with the fantasy storyline of the two movies.

Jenkins's "Recent Sculpture" solo exhibition at Los Angeles's Koslow Gallery (May 1988) featured six maquettes and a life-size installation. Central to all works is Stick Man – an animated figure whose motion relative to his environment is the essence of each piece. *A Constant* is a particularly poetic, yet poignant, work. A lone sailor rows a concrete raft against the overwhelming force of an undulating sea. The mechanics of the piece are exquisite, yet the work's juxtaposition of the minor motion of man within a larger environmental motion is the dominant impression. Similarly intriguing is *Closure Violation,* an investigation of optical illusion. Stick Man holds the uncompleted corner of a square and endlessly tries to close the form, only to be frustrated. Behind him, a two-sided message panel spins and spells through optical illusion the words "AM IMP." Jenkins is exploring two phenomena – "closure" where the eye tends to complete small gaps in familiar geometric forms, and "persistence of vision" where the afterimages of high-speed repetitive exposures cause the eye to combine otherwise separate images. Art is replete with works investigating illusion. By placing Stick Man in the work and making him a helpless victim of the illusion process, Jenkins has added the human element – perhaps reminding us all that we hold only partial ownership of our optical powers.

In *Last Foray,* Stick Man is suspended over a pit and periodically jerked about at the caprice of primitive captors – society holding the individual hostage. Primal pole beating by two Stick Men adds an element of sound, extending *Last Foray* beyond its dimensions, much as native drums announce unseen jungle society.

Jenkins's latest work is about violence, domination, illusion – all addressed through a sculptural language of motion. There is no celebration of machine, nor does motion serve to animate a narrative. Rather,

PHOTO BY CHARLES S. ALLEN, COURTESY KOSLOW GALLERY.

PHOTO BY RUSSEL THURSTON

PHOTO BY JEFF ATHERTON

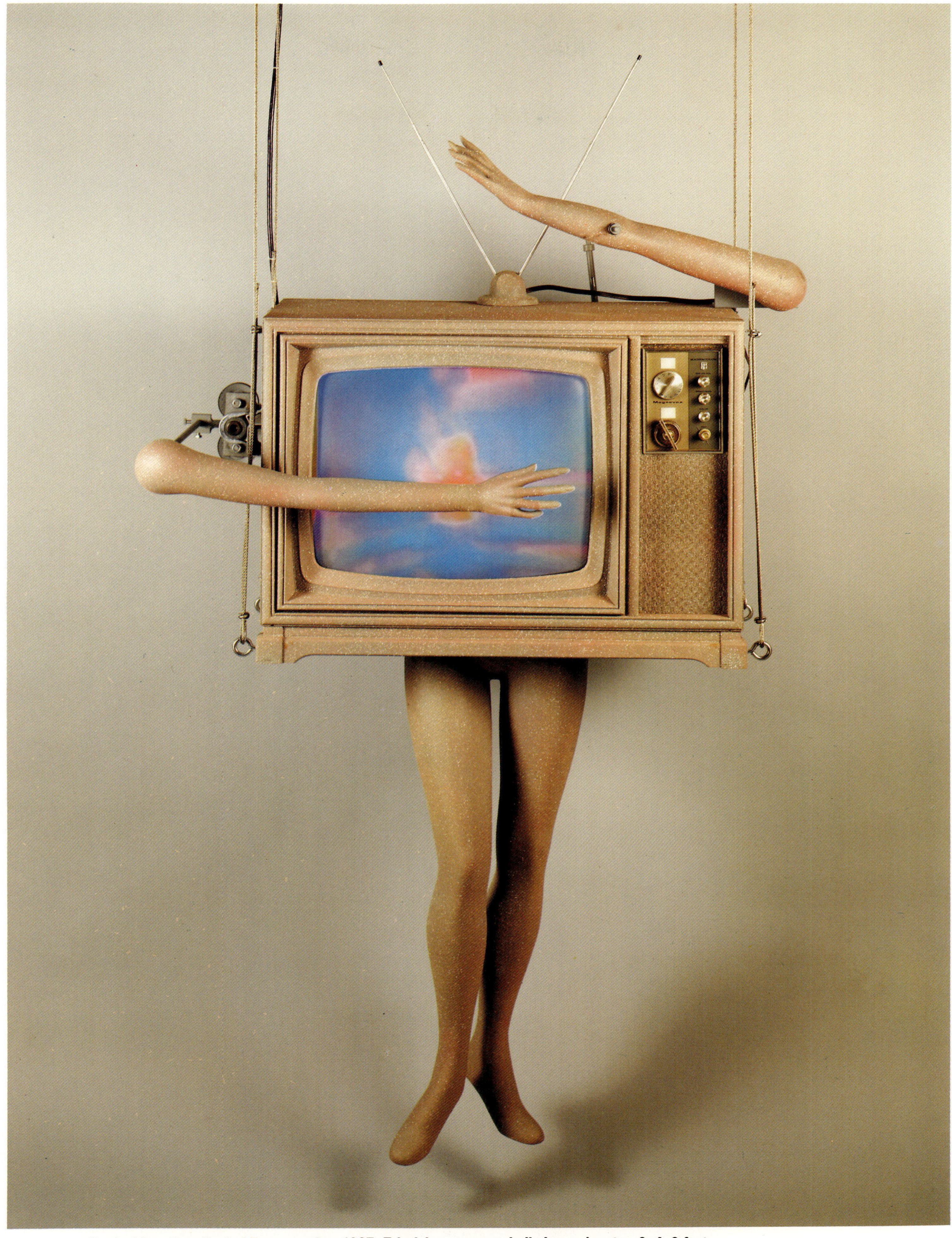

Jim Jenkins, *Coordinated Programming,* 1987. Television, mannequin limbs, and motor. 6x4x3 feet. An operating television set has a pair of animated arms that are motorized so that it rubs its "stomach" and pats its "head." Since the piece is suspended from the ceiling, the momentum of this movement causes the whole piece to twist back and forth.

Jenkins uses motion as an allegory for force – the work is an exploration of forces, those under our control and those beyond our control and how each moment of a moving lifeline is a juxtaposition of the two.

The meek sailor against the mighty sea is a powerful metaphor of the individual's ability to exert only minimal influence over the larger forces that swirl around him – a world in constant motion.

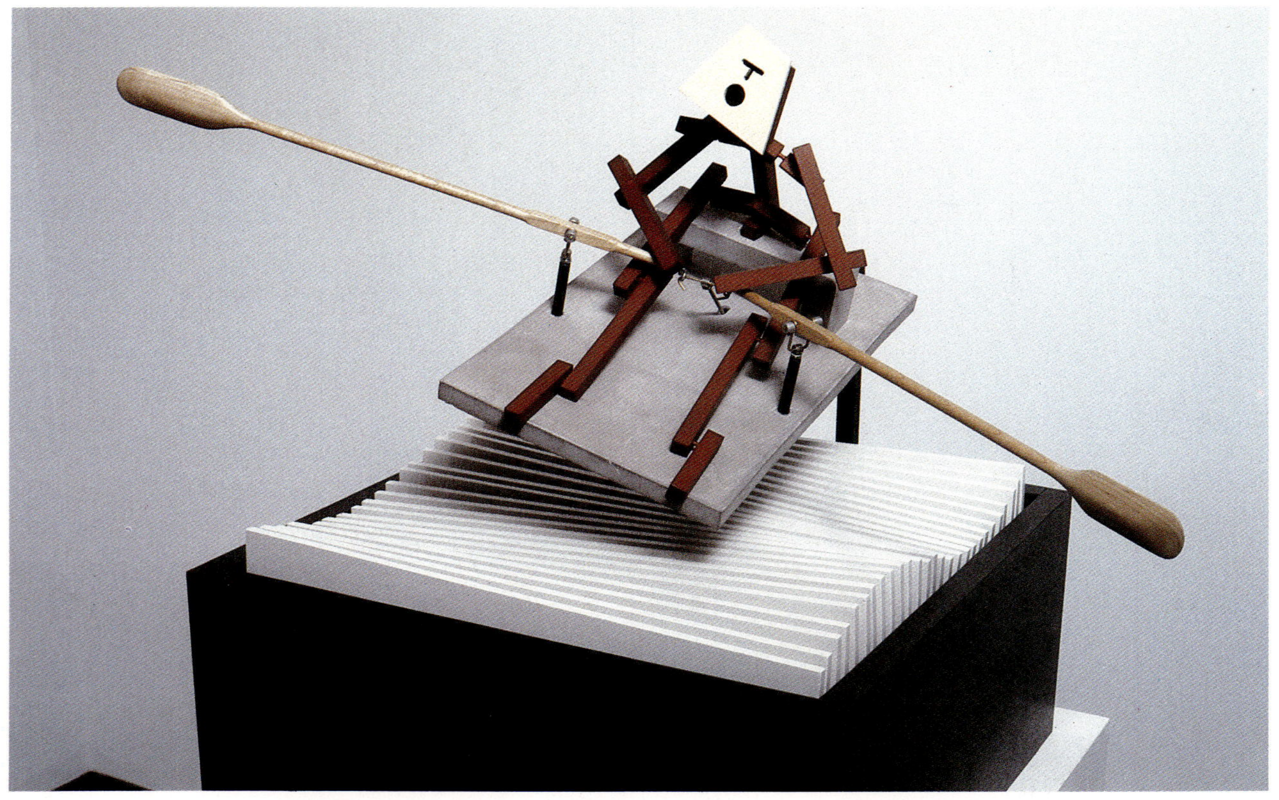

Jim Jenkins, *A Constant,* 1988. Mixed media and motors. 20x26x16 inches.
A stick sailor rows a concrete raft against the immense force of the sea.

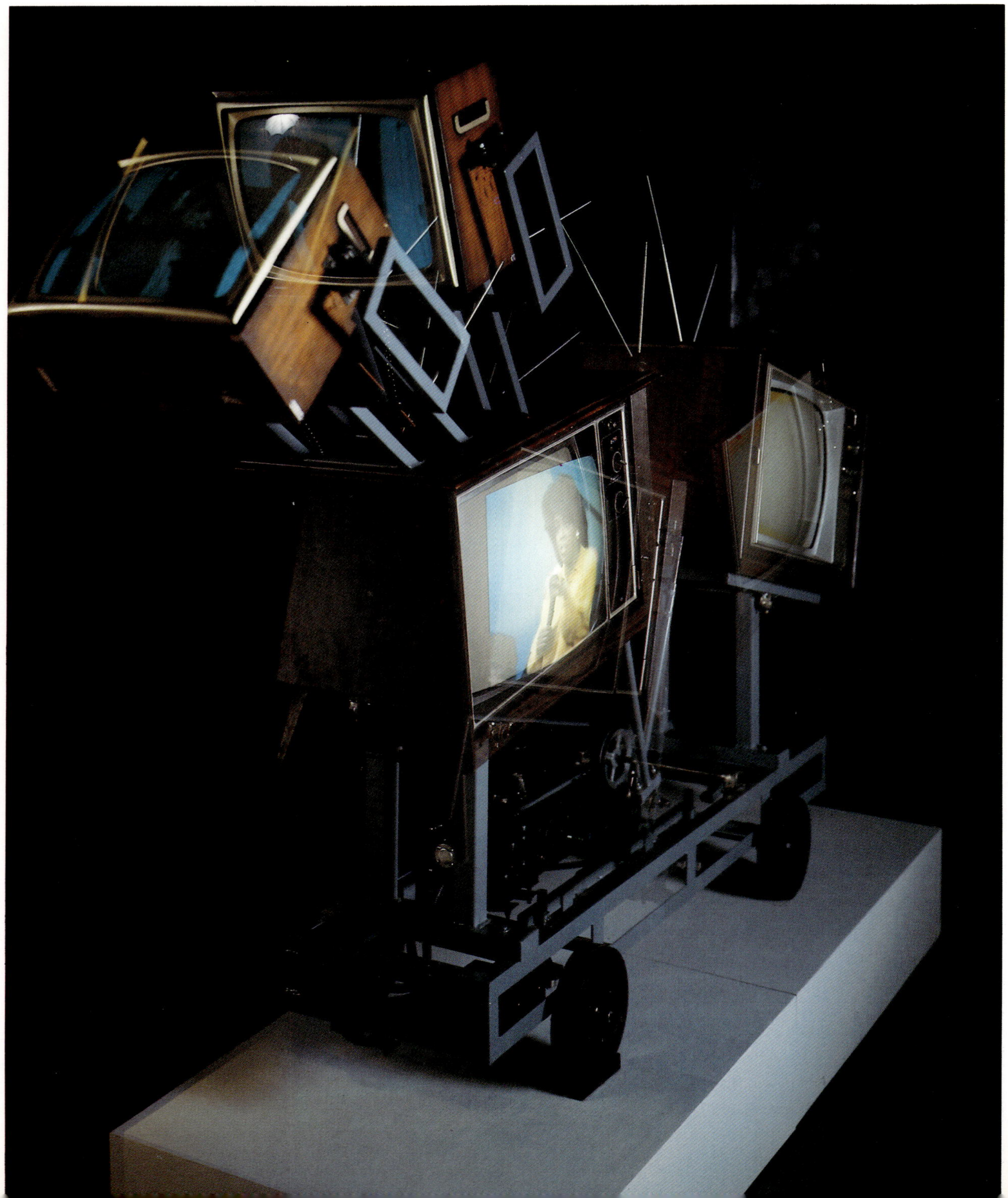

PHOTO BY STEVE LAVOIE

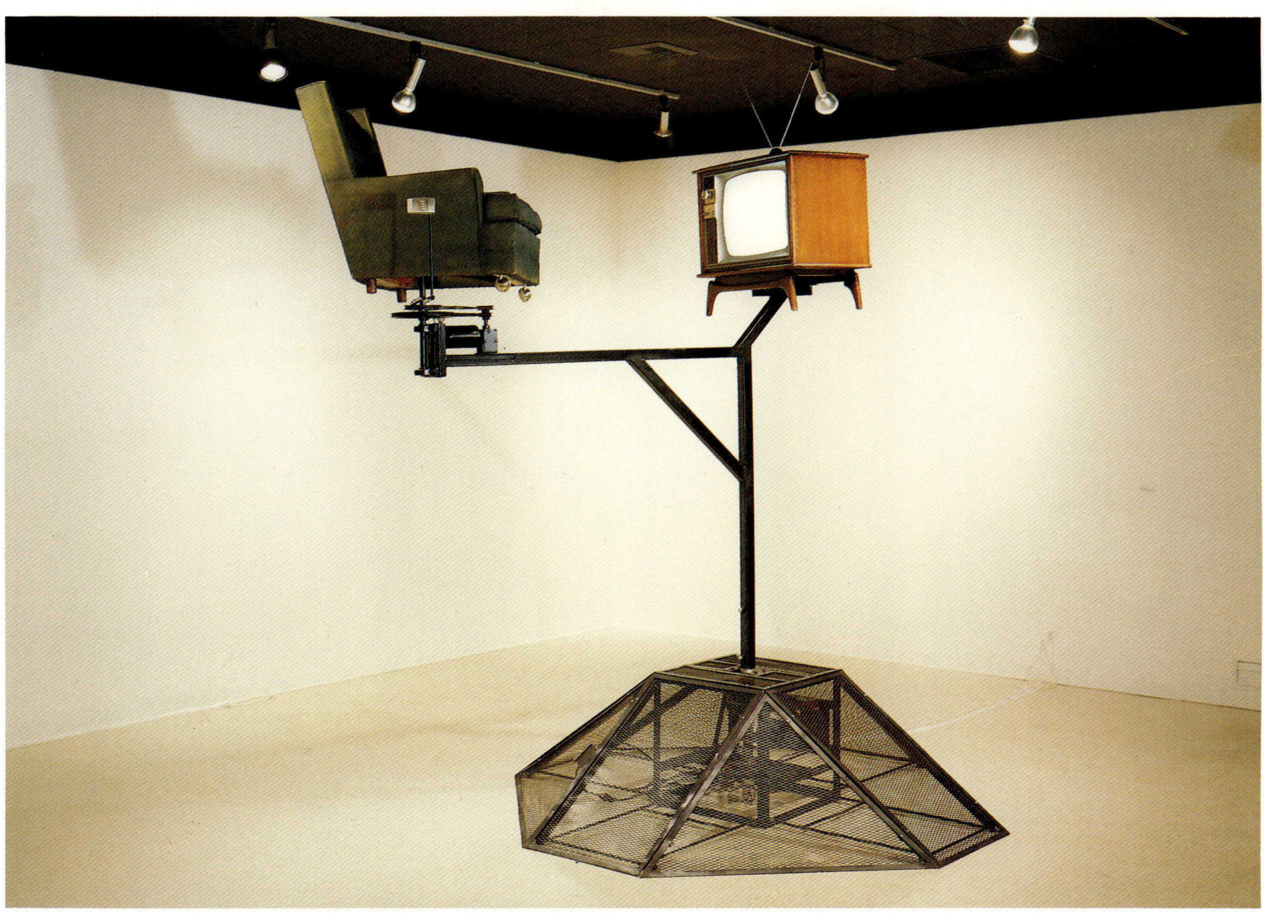

PHOTO BY STEVE LAVOIE

Jim Jenkins, ***As the World Turns,*** **1984. Television, chair steel, and motors. TV, chair, and remote control spin around in a commentary on our soap opera universe.**

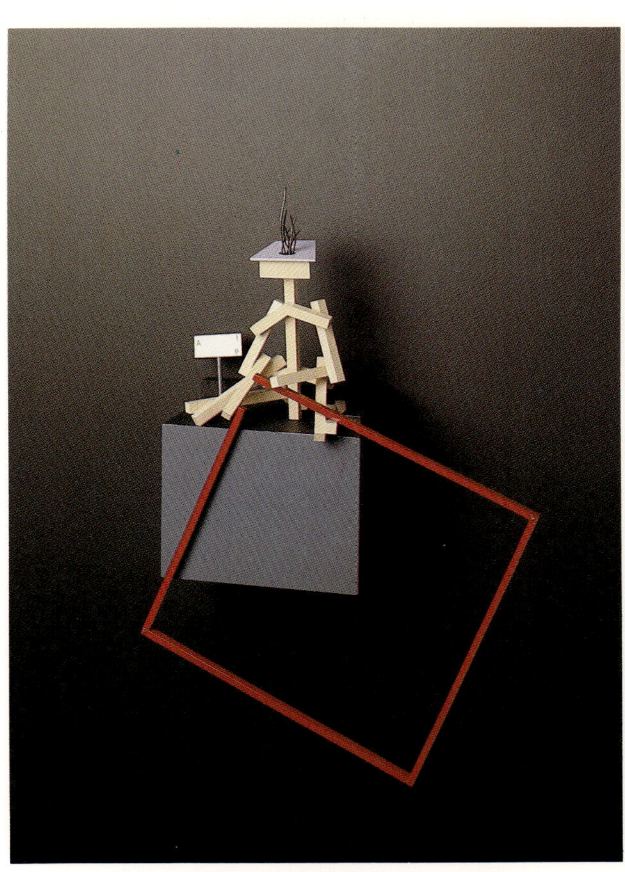

PHOTOS BY CHARLES S. ALLEN

Jim Jenkins, ***Closure Violation,*** **1988.**
A stick man tries endlessly without success to close the corner of the square.

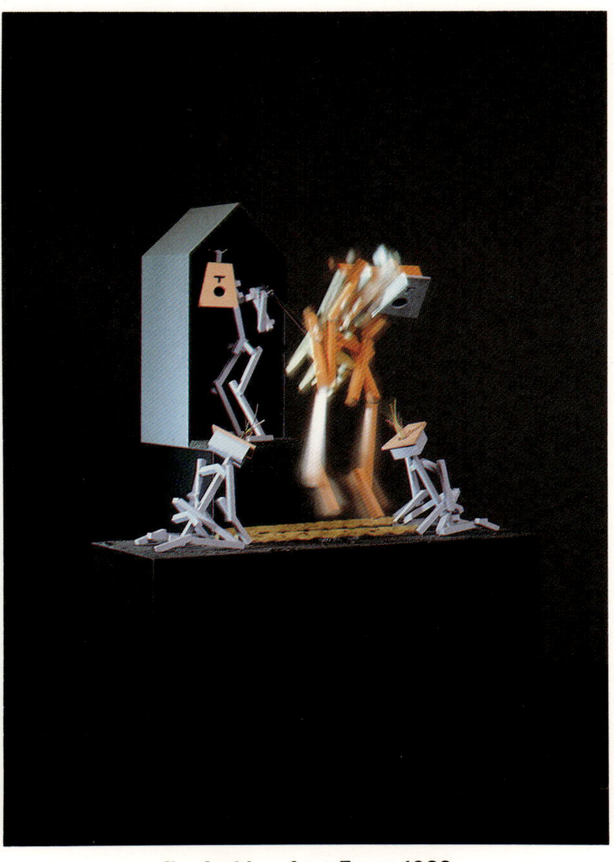

Jim Jenkins, ***Last Foray,*** **1988.**
An orange figure sits in a chair suspended over a hole. A standing figure intermittently shakes the chair. Two kneeling figures pound a pair of poles in rhythm.

Facing page, Jim Jenkins, ***Video Rodeo,*** **1986. Televisions, steel, motors. A bucking bronc made of television sets.**

Gary Justis

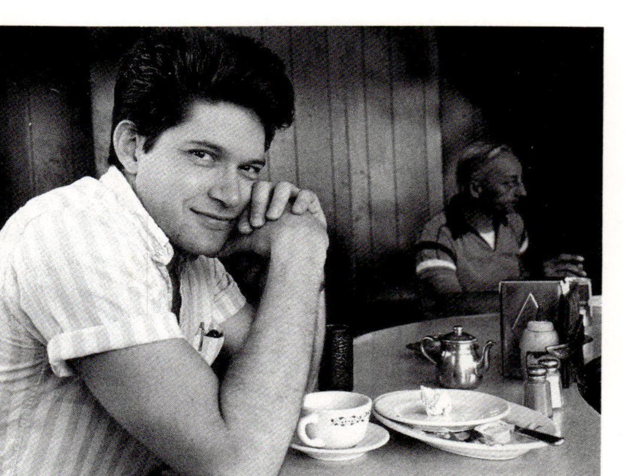

JOANNE CUBBS, CURATOR AT WISCONSIN's Kohler Arts Center, selected Gary Justis's *Chromosome* for the catalog cover photo of the landmark 1987 "Eccentric Machines" exhibition. The exhibition featured twenty artists who incorporate movement into their work and even within this group of select peers, the sculpture of Gary Justis stands unique.

Justis builds machines. They are machine-for-the-sake-of-machine. Void of traditional function, Justis's sculptures are the hybrid composite of twentieth-century industrial materials in search of the truths of fundamental sculptural form. Yes, the machines are assembled. Yet there is almost no real sense of assemblage – the minutia of individual elements are so cleanly coordinated into the work that they simply fit as a whole. As a whole, the works are very gestural, biomorphic, with fluid graceful lines foreign to machine, even foreign to their own hard industrial materials. The sum is very poetic. Point, line, plane, and motion merge into coherent statement. Justis is clearly in control of his art – perhaps nowhere can be found a more truthful expression of machine-as-extension-of-human.

According to Justis, *Chromosome* "came out of a dream I had about making a machine that would project your genes into the future... humanity's main objective."

With the topic of DNA and the double helix – the fundamental commonality of all life on Earth of all time – Justis works in metaphorical territory as central to Man's universe as the Greek's basic elements of Earth, Air, Wind, Water, and Fire. Yet the double helix is a topic denied all preceding generations of artists who, in tandem with pre-1950 science, could only guess the atomic mechanics of life-form renewal.

Eight feet in height, *Chromosome* looms over the viewer and exudes energy – both potential and kinetic. It is a work about the milieu of forces within which all life swims: the steady human-scale force of gravity against which *Chromosome* stands eight feet tall; the far more intense electromagnetic force which drives *Chromosome*'s motors, bright lights, and many of the machines of Man; and the unimaginably awesome nuclear force (first awakened by Human at Alamogordo in 1945) that is the stuff binding all atoms including the nucleotides of DNA.

Three separate motions drive *Chromosome.* At the base, twin cables on twin motors twist in awkward symmetry – a direct visual reference to the double helix given life by Justis's movement just as the double helix itself gives life to all living form. Further up *Chromosome*'s precarious aluminum spine, two wooden dowels repeat the double helix motif. Attached to high-speed motors, the dowels spin and blur into two translucent spheroids allegorical to the "shadow prints" of complex atoms produced by a science that can only view the greatly magnified reflections of the double helix, not the atom itself. A third motion, an intense slide projector light and high-speed muffin fan, periodically vibrate *Chromosome* seemingly in reference to the magically violent moment when the chromosome splits – the universal essence of renewal of all life-forms.

Chromosome is an imposing allegory about life. It is executed in a hard functionalism, a sort of "pseudo-aircraft" technology which answers to the god of strength-to-weight ratio. Aluminum, nylon fittings, and tubed wiring create a consistent language with intense economy – a powerful reenactment of the incredible information storage economy the double helix represents, and a reminder that all life itself is the

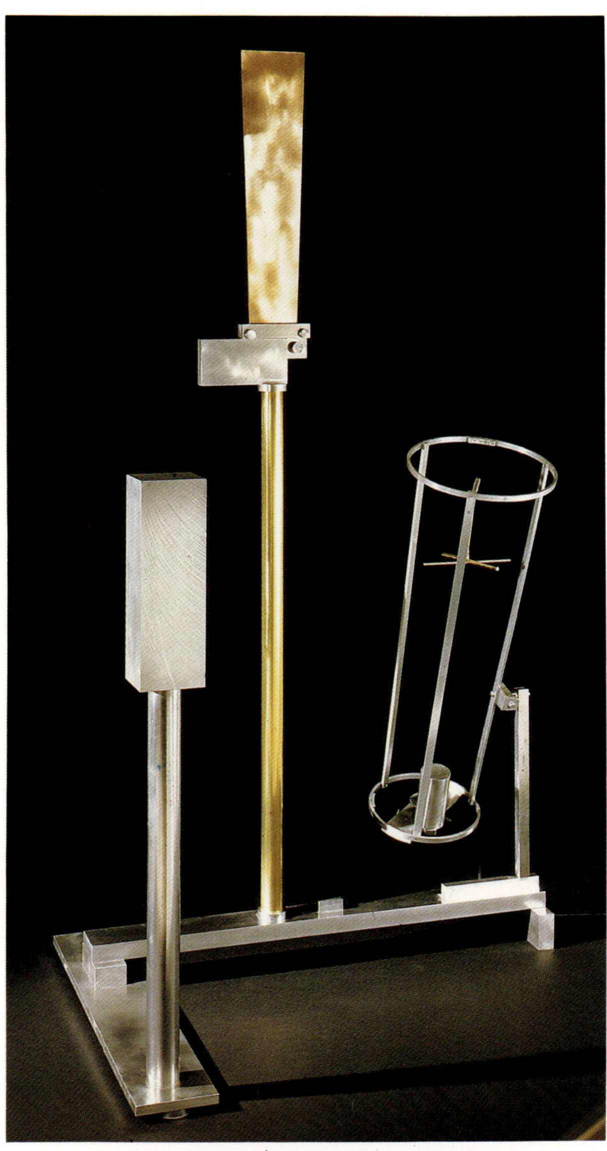

PHOTO BY STEVEN GROSS

Gary Justis, *Untitled,* (vessel) 1988.
Aluminum and brass. This piece has a cagelike structure attached on the right side that tilts back and forth very slowly. At the same time, a brass element, representing the tendency of a liquid to stay level, maintains its own level orientation with the floor.

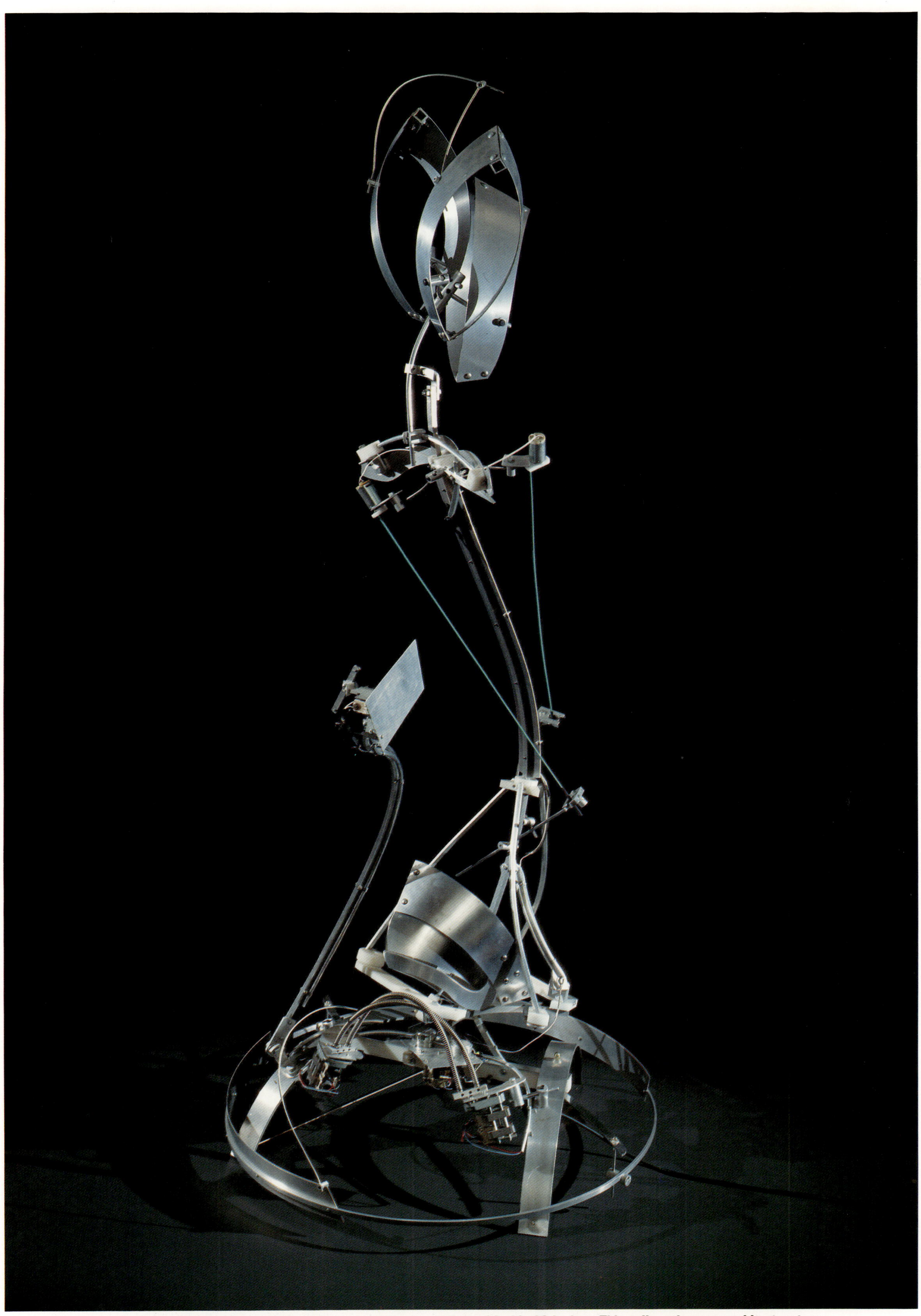

Gary Justis, *Chromosome,* 1986. Aluminum, motors, and light. 98x40x40 inches. This tall, anthropomorphic structure has a pair of thin, blue strips of wood that rapidly spin, causing them to bow outward. A strobe flashes onto them in motion and gives the illusion of forming complete teardrop-shaped volumes.

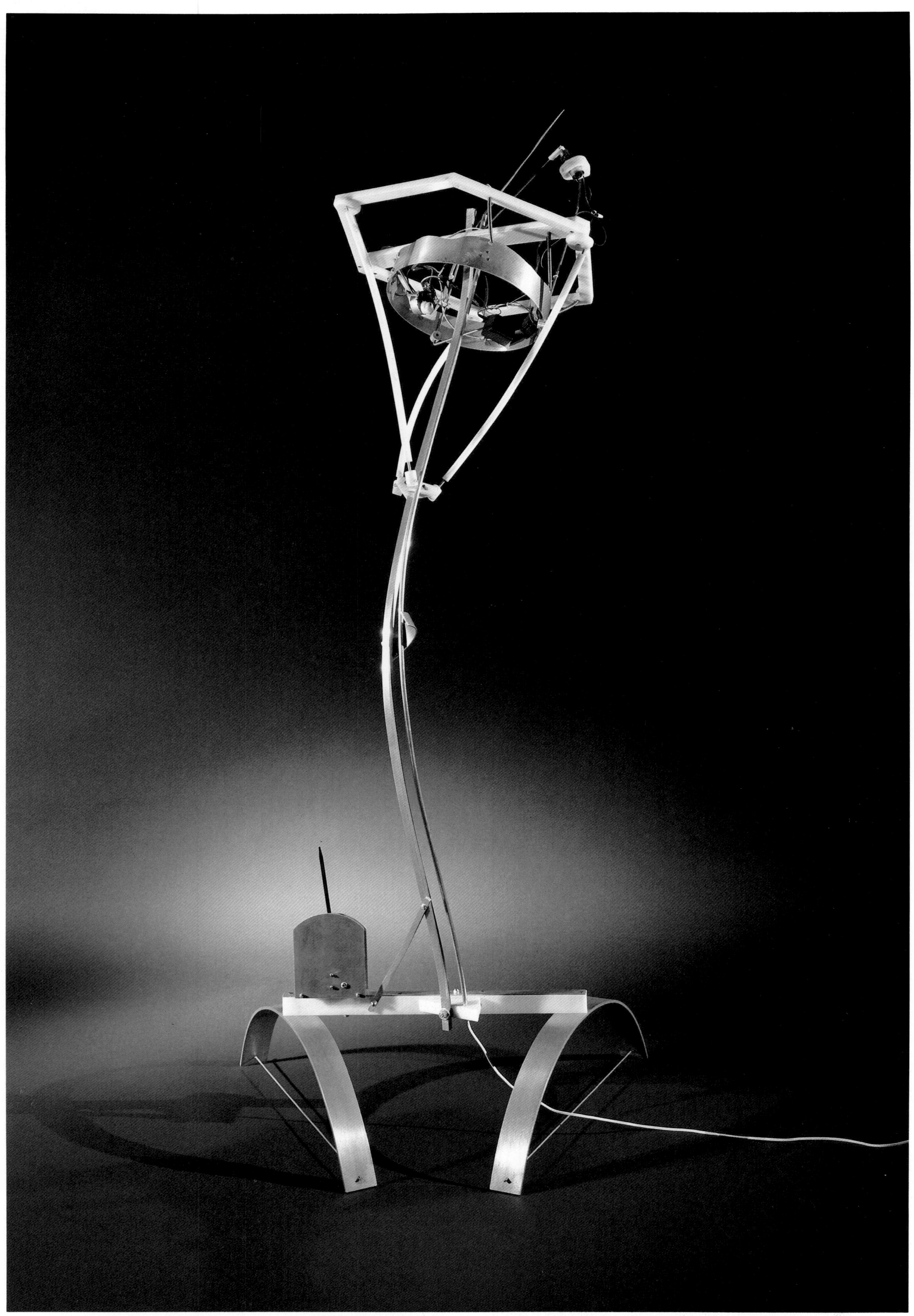

Gary Justis, *Controlled Stamen,* 1986. Plastic, aluminum, and motor. 82x28x33 inches. While a metronome marks time on the base of the piece, the stamenlike piece atop the assemblage pulsates.

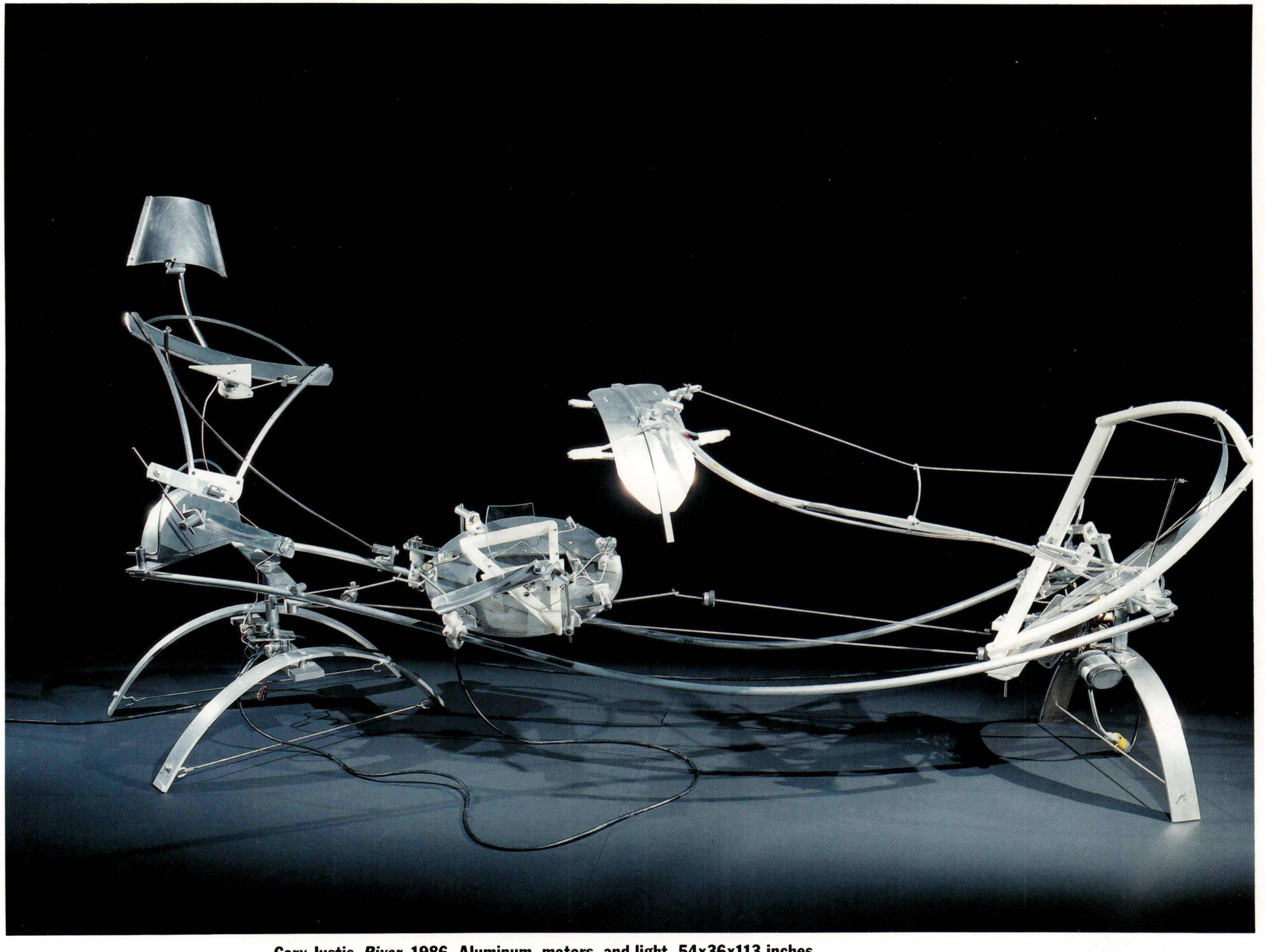

Gary Justis, *River,* 1986. Aluminum, motors, and light. 54x36x113 inches. This beautifully crafted work features a central moving carriage that slides back and forth along a pair of rails. The carriage pivots and twists during this process, reflecting a neon light hidden within the structure above.

assemblage of inorganic materials and energy borrowed from the Cosmos.

A second biomorphic work of similar dimensions is *Controlled Stamen,* which stands on a vertical axis over six feet tall. Like *Chromosome,* this work investigates the diverse language of motion – a metronome beats constant time at the base of the work. Randomly, the stamen assembly atop the work shudders into movement as if ejecting its reproductive arsenal under the scrutiny of time-lapse photography. Rather than a rendering, *Stamen* is abstract allegory to the randomness of genetic creation. No matter how in control Man and his science seek to be, all individuals are conceived prior to their control and live a lifetime under the umbrella of millions of random microgenetic pairings along the length of the double helix.

Justis moves from life topic to water motion with *River.* True to its title, *River's* frenzied motion is along its horizontal axis – a complex flexing trolley on irregular rails with a glass pane that unevenly reflects neon light above it. The motion is highly erratic, high speed, driven by free-floating dual independent cable-driven motion. Anyone who has ever stared at length at a single point in a rushing river will understand *River's* visual reference – the ceaseless motion of light through infinite transparent rivulets. *River* evokes a range of water-related images by abstract reference. Again, Justis's machine provides metaphorical replication of natural phenomenon.

When asked how he became involved with motion, Justis states that he has never thought of kinetics as a novelty art form, but a "very natural evolutionary process." The 1960s rise (and fall?) of kinetic art was, in Justis's view, "an art-science gee-whiz approach – phenomenological." Justis has seen the 1980s as a time conducive to a more narrative, metaphoric investigation of machines. "Machines have become more taken for granted in the last twenty years. The use of narrative brings machines closer, allows the investigation of spirituality."

Justis's investigations exude an inner truth, a pristine search for machine context akin to art's many millennia search for the ideal human form. By organizing inorganic materials into seemingly living form, Justis is mimicking a billion-year process of life's evolution. After all, life itself is only the organization of inorganic materials stolen from the entropy of the Universe.

By Justis's view, the time is right for art to steal the machine from science. According to Justis, "Art versus science and art will always win since science lives within its own limitations. Art has none."

Robert Mark Packer

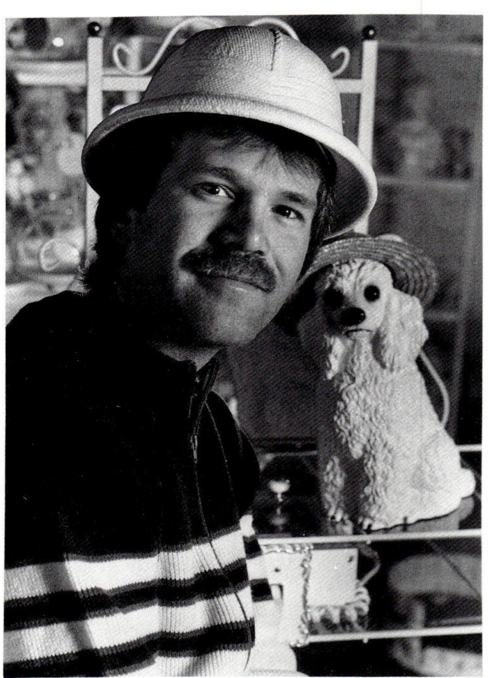

PHOTO BY KRISTINE DITTMER

BITING SOCIAL COMMENTARY AND caustic wit drive the unconventional work of Michigan artist Robert Mark Packer. On the surface, Packer's work is joyfully constructed fun. With all humor of substance there is a target, a victim, and Packer takes direct aim at lost individuality in mass culture. By creating an art statement that is persistently irreverent of the established art order, Packer becomes his own metaphor for a broader attack upon the established order of society as a whole.

One of Packer's most recent works, *The Tomb of King Too-Much-In-Common,* is a diorama parody of ancient Egypt's Valley of the Pharaohs. Visualizing the cliche of Egyptian slaves as nameless ants in a highly ordered insect society, Packer's *Tomb* contains 200 living harvester ants in eager coexistence with a buxom sphinx constructed of fifty-three pounds of orange candy. The sands of ancient Egypt literally become ant farm turf, and munching the orange sugar sphinx provides sustenance for ants as did working the orange sandstone of the real sphinx for slaves. Packer's *Tomb* weaves an entire aberrant Egyptian fantasy – ants work in the shadow of an illustrated pyramid backdrop (reminiscent of turn-of-the-century box camera photographer bogus travel-shot backdrops). The tomb edifice itself is humorously detailed in two-dimensional relief showing ant-feelered gods and ant body-inspired pseudohieroglyphics. Movement is subtle (only the scurrying of live harvester ants and flickering flame light bulbs) and is appropriately scaled to the dwarf dimension of Man as he moves about the real Valley of the Pharaohs.

Hari Kari Ketchup King (front cover) is perhaps Packer's most celebrated work. Conceived and constructed while an artist-in-residence in Roswell, New Mexico, *Ketchup King* displays a pyramid of fifty-three tiered tomatoes (either real or plastic tomatoes depending upon the display circumstance) each slashing itself with a motorized razor blade. Two Chairman Mao Tomato portraits dominate the work. Japanese Rising Sun flags are replaced by Rising Tomatoes. Banners, lanterns, pagodas, and golden dragons festoon the hacking tomato hordes. A miniature public address system broadcasts Chinese folk tunes set to disco music and completes the absurd parody. *Hari Kari Ketchup King* purposely confuses two great Asian cultures (Chinese and Japanese) – a soft cultural slur by an Occidental artist who reminds us that not only is the individual lost within mass culture, but cultures themselves can become muddled and lost in the eyes of contemporary outsiders and future historians.

Packer's rapier satire takes aim at religion and the

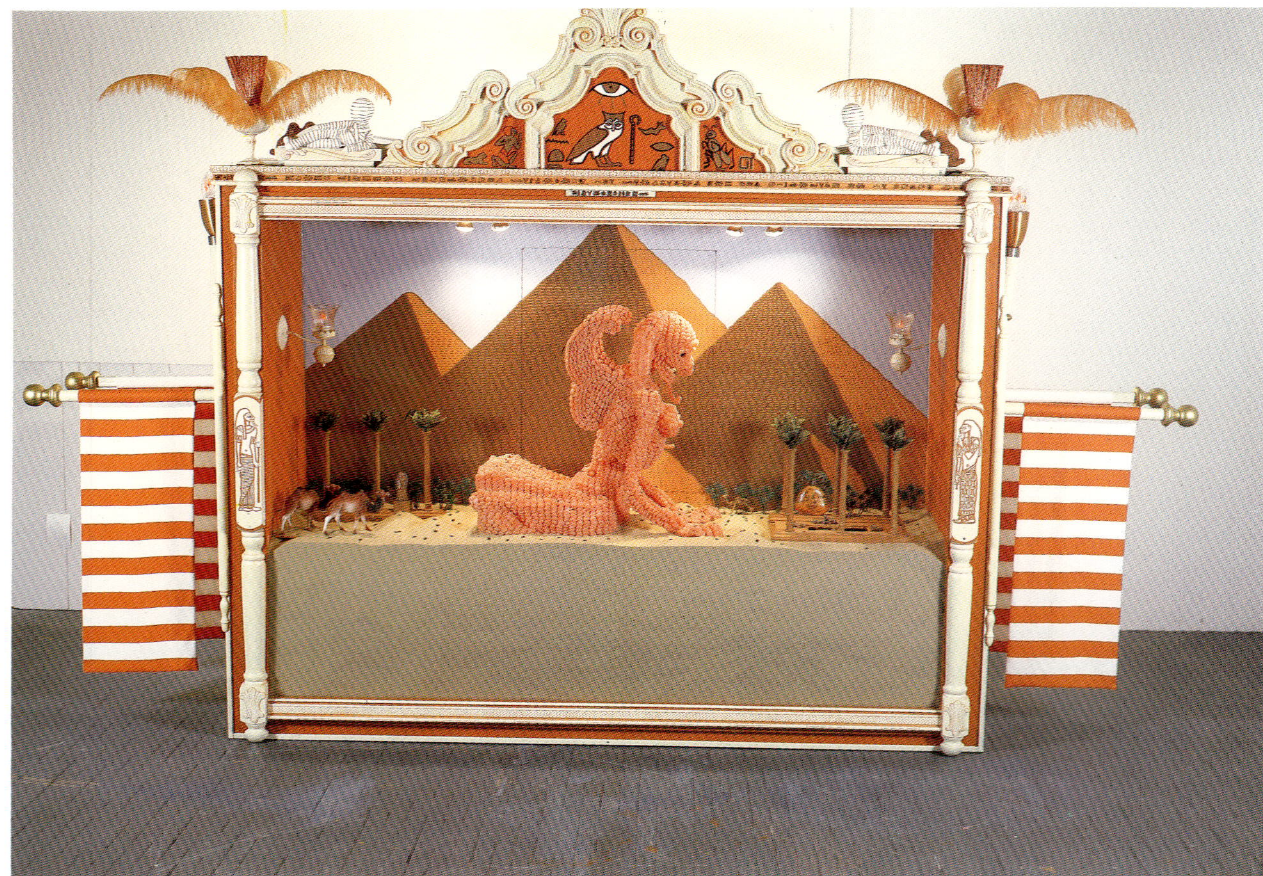

Robert Mark Packer, *The Tomb of King Too-Much-In-Common,* 1987 – 88. Wood, plastic, and mixed media. 9x12x2 feet. In a large-scale Egyptian-style ant farm, a colony of live ants feeds upon the pink sugar sphinx and creates a complex system of tunnels inside this "tomb."

extravaganza of cathedral funerals in *The Transcendental Model Isn't Dead – It Just Smells Funny.* A congregation of brilliant white onions contrasts with the dark blue church installation appointments. A vaporizer filled with pulverized onions assaults the viewer, bringing tears to the eyes in mockery of the sentimentality that may be core to organized religion. In accompaniment to baroque church music, a winged onion rises from the coffin and ascends to the heavens – a vegetative travesty reenactment of the Holy Resurrection in a gaudy church where the onion masses see their Deity in their own likeness, as does man.

Painstaking detail and superb design, kinetic and graphic execution lend credence to Packer's otherwise wildly irreverent portfolio. Thematic constants include high consistency of theme within each work, and the organization of a plethora of individual elements into a coherent overall composition. From a distance, the installations are enticing and their movement and detail command the viewer to make closer inspection. The language of Packer's art is richly varied and includes: assemblage of found objects ("my art is driven by the 'found object'. . . . There is no greater joy than finding the right object on the store shelf"); extravaganza (an admitted devotee of Busby Berkeley); humor (both lowbrow pun and high-energy satire and parody); skilled illustration; the constant use of living (or just plucked) objects (e.g., fish, sagebrush, tomatoes, onions, chameleons, ants, hot dogs); and, of course, movement.

While a graduate student at the Art Institute of Chicago, Packer investigated classical sculpture and the affects of time – how marble went from raw to finished, then continued to change as it aged far beyond the lifetime of its sculptor. It is the vulnerability of all art. The issue is not change, but merely rate of change. When Packer uses perishables such as onions or tomatoes, he is really just using the classical's raw marble with a much shorter half life, accelerating the law of entropy – a law which inevitably will deny art's historical pursuit of immortality. Egypt's heralded Sphinx, slowly disintegrating sandstone (whose nose was blown off by Napoleon's army during cannon practice), becomes fifty-three pounds of orange candy whose "movement" is merely faster than that of sandstone.

Why the preoccupation with Man's relationship to mass culture? Packer is a rust belt resident, and he describes his homeland as "the birthplace of mass production and mass marketing." Beneath the clever wit and baroque execution, Packer's work is built upon a bedrock of cultural, social, and political poignancy. By creating parodies of mass cultures from afar, Packer challenges industrial culture to investigate itself. Is the nameless Egyptian slave any more anonymous than the modern average citizen of the industrial world who will bequeath to future millennia behemoth freeway cloverleafs and high-rise pyramids?

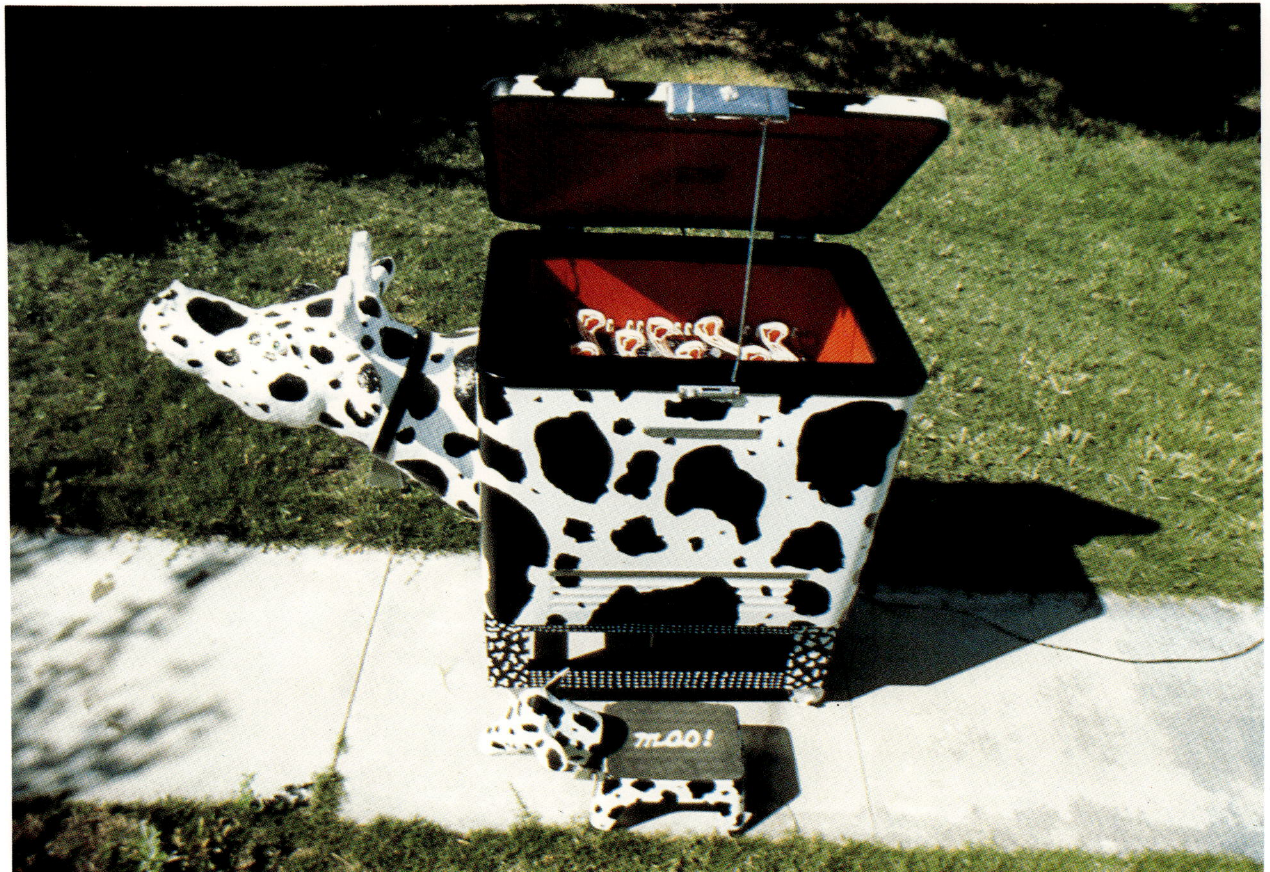

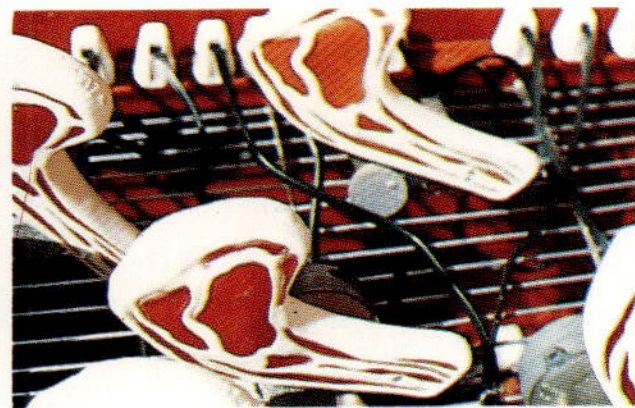

Robert Mark Packer, *The Fall of the House of Udder,* 1984. Metal, wood, and plastic. 5x6x3 feet. A working freezer on a rolling cart with bovine attachments looks like a Holstein cow. The viewer steps up on the back of the 'calf' and opens the lid of the freezer/cow. Inside, twenty-four vinyl steaks bob up and down erratically, squeaking and honking pathetically.

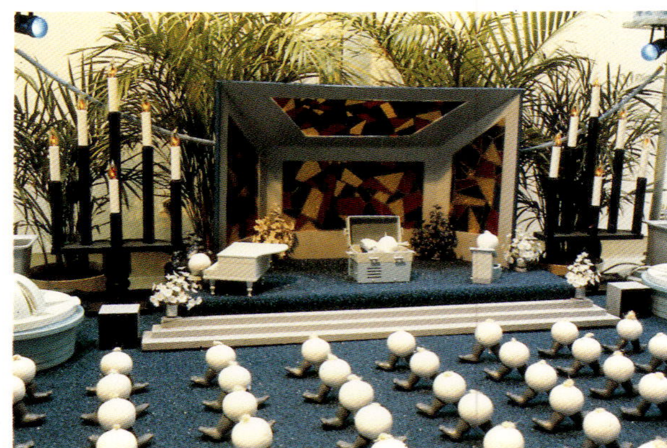

Robert Mark Packer, *The Transcendental Model Isn't Dead—It Just Smells Funny,* 1984. Mixed media. 10x8x8 feet. A crowd of onions sit in neat rows facing a 10-foot crucifix. An onion pianist and an onion preacher flank a coffin. At each corner of the platform is a stand topped by a box of tissues and a waste basket. Vaporizers spray a fine mist of onion juice onto the viewers while speakers play a soundtrack of Protestant hymns and a white winged onion rises from the coffin.

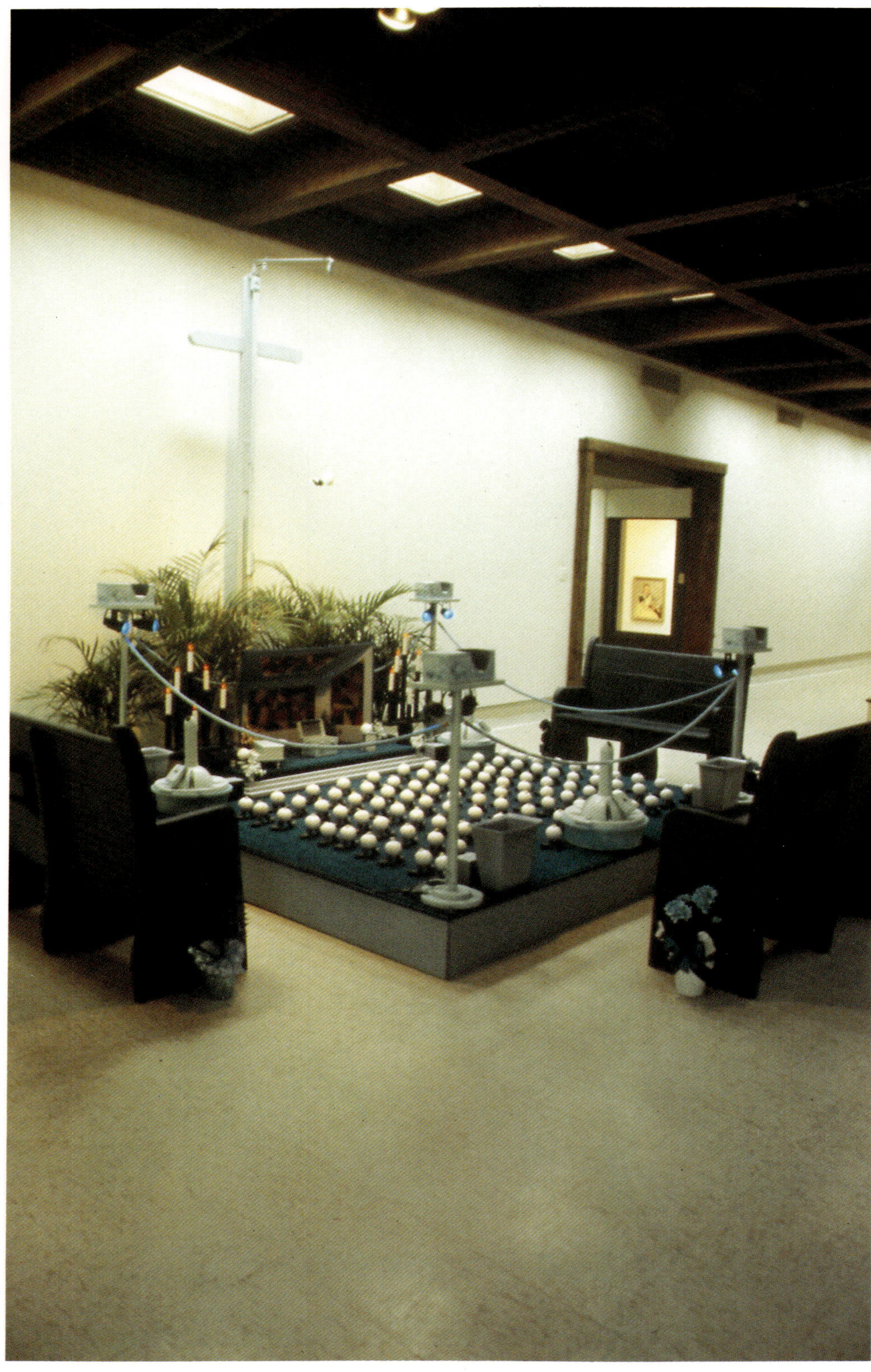

Robert Mark Packer, *Ein Grüner Greisengarten (The Old Green Folks Home),* 1984. Plywood, enamel, and mixed media. 5x8x8 feet. A combination refrigeration case and hospital/sanitarium is home to twenty small wheelchairs and walkers occupied by various vegetables. The vegetables struggle around the green astroturf, illuminated by banks of fluorescent lights and cooled by refrigerated air blown from the building. The soundtrack contains electronic rhythms and counting in German. Actual intravenous feeding of BHT and water preserves the inhabitants.

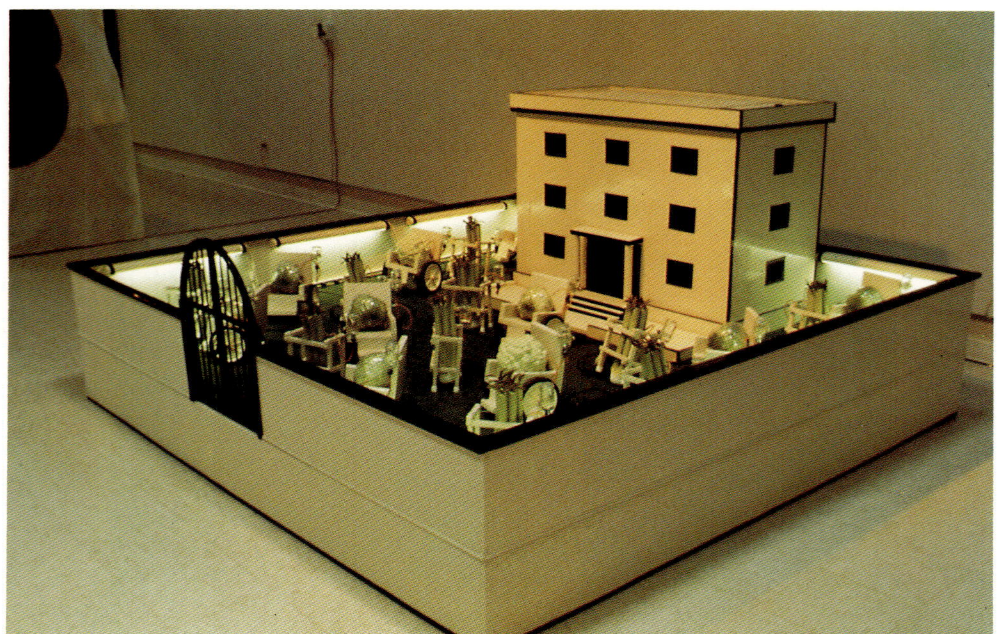

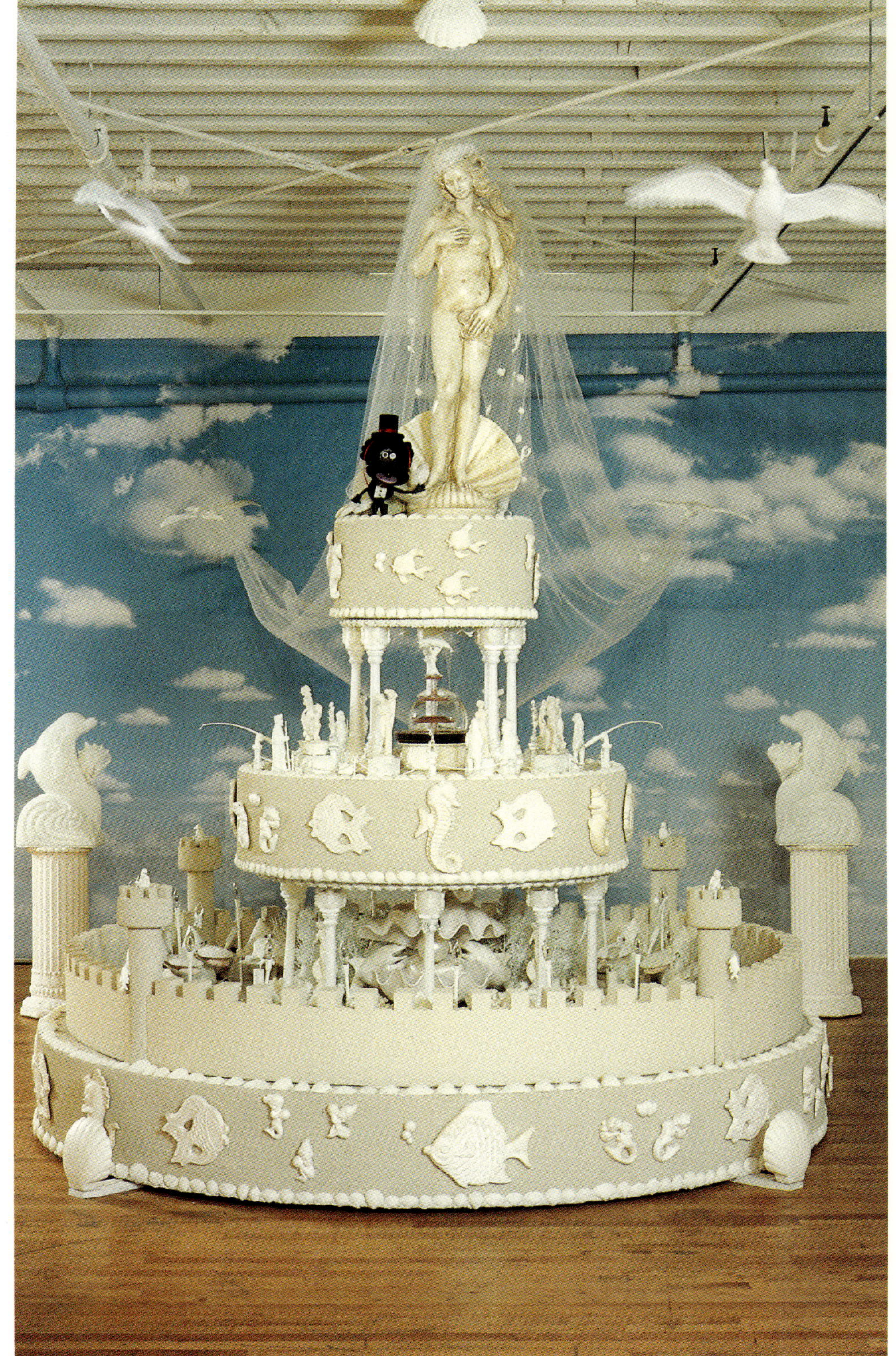

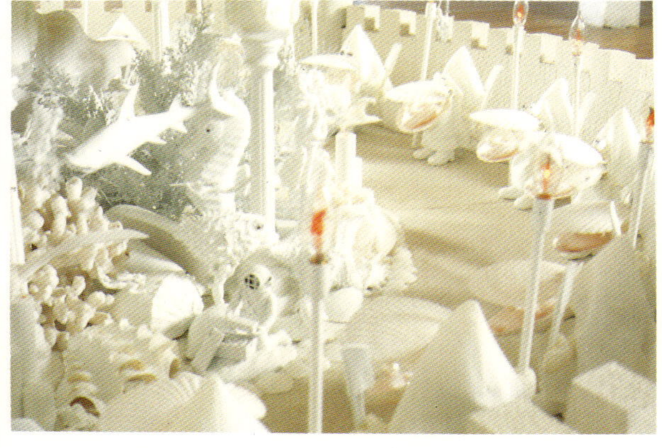

Robert Mark Packer, *She Sells Sea Shells by the Superhighway,* 1985–86. Styrofoam, sand, and mixed media. 11x11x17 feet. The bridegroom, a small animated clam, sings a rap tune to the bride, a 100-pound cast concrete Venus. Sea gulls twirl overhead, a series of multicolored disco lights illuminate the cake, and a second soundtrack of pounding surf mixed with Glenn Miller's "String of Pearls" emanates from large conch shells held by two illuminated dolphins. A small fountain on the middle tier is activated intermittently. The action climaxes when twenty-one white clams bearing flickering torches open up gradually, revealing their pearls in unison. A photomural behind the sculpture completes the tableau.

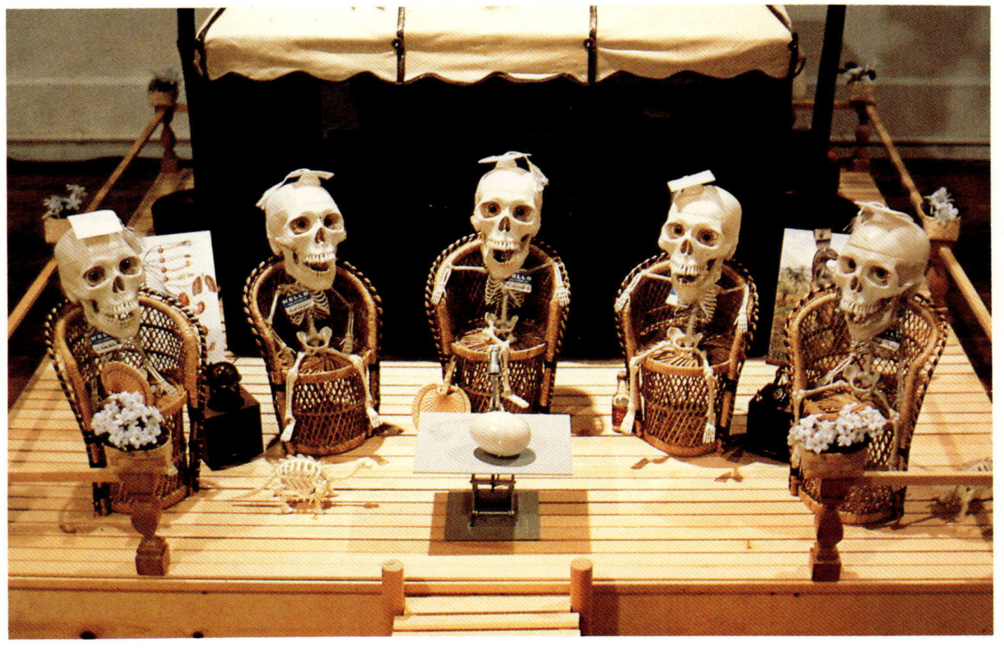

Robert Mark Packer, *The Egg at Knee and the Eggs That See (The Strange Case of Shimmelfarbus Canopenerus),* 1984–85. Mixed media. 6x6x7 feet. Dr. Shimmelfarbus and his colleagues have found and reconstructed the skeleton of a prehistoric creature. The five academicians, also in skeleton form, sing in unison to a soundtrack of pygmy and West African folk songs and Mitch Miller's "Ramona," while an egg from the creature rocks gently to and fro on a small examination table.

Bryan Rogers

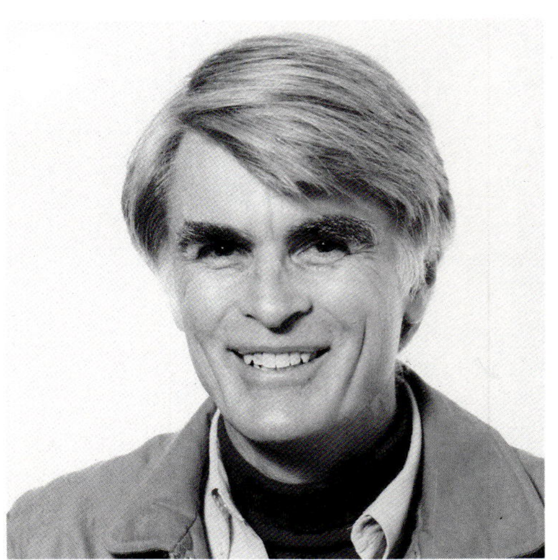

FEW ARTISTS CAN CLAIM THE DUBIous distinction of having been reviewed by yellow journalism's *National Enquirer,* whose 29 July 1980 issue headlined: "Goldfish Harpooned to Death in Disgusting 'Work of Art.' " The review described a "mindless exhibit" on display at California State University at Hayward, which featured a sculpture that automatically harpooned a steel spear into an aquarium within which swam one lone goldfish. The work of art was entitled *A Matter of Time.* It was inspired by the fast reaction time of the fish, and the fact that the spear always moved slower than the fish's previously measured reaction time.

As fate would have it, in the midst of all the controversy, the goldfish died, although not by the point of the spear, but of natural causes. A second victim of the entire ordeal was its author, artist Bryan Rogers. Rogers, now Chairman of the Art Department at Carnegie-Mellon University in Pittsburgh, fell under scrutiny of the SPCA and was inundated with a flurry of letters and telephone calls from around the country, all of which were reprimanding the artist for his violent tendency to create machines of torture for small, helpless animals.

This memorable incident was an isolated one within Rogers's career. Rogers diverted to an art career through the field of chemical engineering. While completing his doctorate work at the University of California at Berkeley, Rogers first discovered art as a "visual alternative to creative brain work." Utilizing his engineering background, Rogers set out to create a body of work that coupled the sophistication of science and electronics with the visually questioning concept of art. He chose to investigate the umbrella. Applying research techniques that would rival NASA, Rogers began to thoroughly draw, dissect, isolate, and animate umbrellas. Although the artist claims that the choice of this object was purely coincidental, these investigations have remained steady, though not exclusive, from the onset in the early seventies until a major solo exhibition of fifty umbrellas at the Portland Contemporary Crafts Gallery in 1988.

In an article written by the artist for the *Leonardo* journal in 1975, he describes the use of the umbrella:

> *Originally I had no intention of developing a series or of working with a single specified object as a continuing reference. But the umbrella helped me to do both. Initially an experimental addition which I made to a*

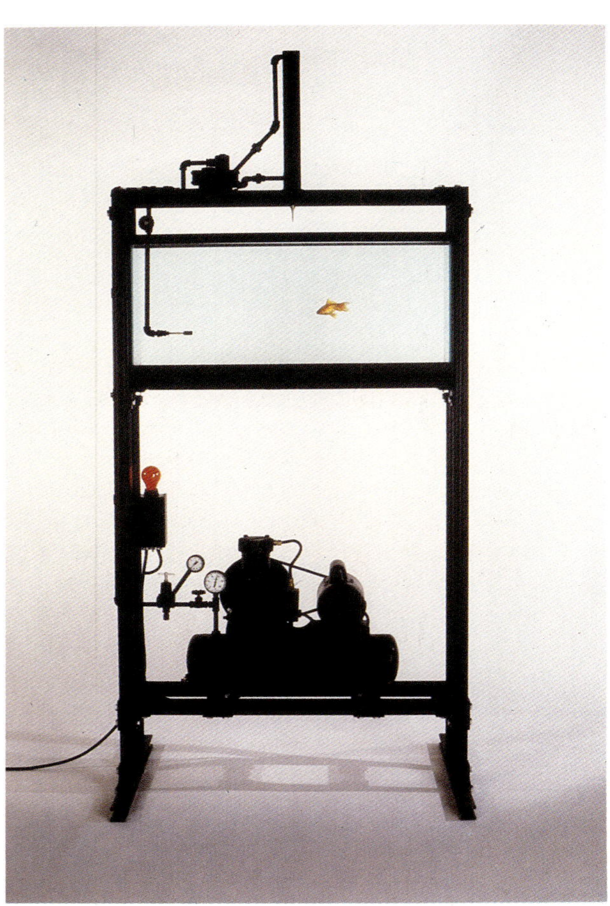

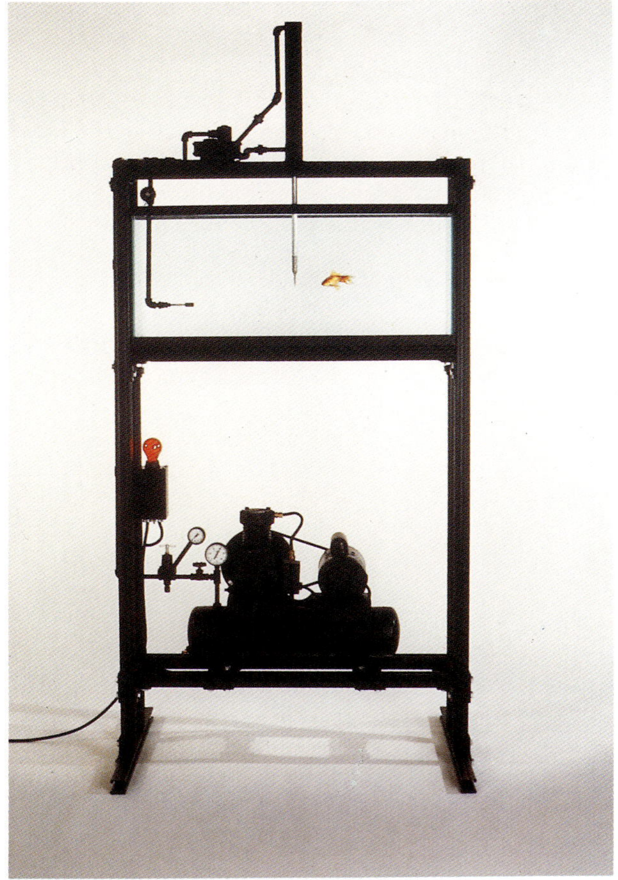

PHOTOS BY JOE SAMBERG

Bryan Rogers, *A Matter of Time,* 1977. Live goldfish, water, glass tank, compressor, pneumatic cylinder, timer, steel framing, hardware. 88x42x30 inches. Periodically the pneumatic cylinder mounted above the tank thrusts the sharpened piston into the water.

machine, the umbrella began to serve me in the same manner as a canvas serves a painter: it became a format to which I could return again and again, thus avoiding the difficulty of starting from zero with each new work. It was a tool, a continually available material starting point. I found that its use eventually set up possibilities for a self-referent system. That is, working only with the "idea" of umbrella began to seem consistent.

An umbrella is not only a common, functional object of intricate construction, it also has an elegant geometrical form. Yet, it does not seem to be an appropriate object to be taken seriously from the point of view of art. It was, however, this contrasting aspect of an umbrella that became the key to the door between my artistic interests and my technical knowledge and skills. The umbrella facilitated my working with the nonsense possibilities, both of machines and of scientific ideas and methods.

One of the earliest of these works, dating from 1973, is a work entitled *Machine to Move an Umbrella Up and Down.* With all components exposed, the work consists of a permanently open umbrella which has a mechanism hooked up to the base of its shaft. When activated, the motor spins a gear, which, in turn, raises and lowers the umbrella. In another work from the same year entitled *Umbrella Evacuation Chamber,* a closed umbrella is periodically subjected to vacuum conditions. One of the most elaborate of the early umbrella works, is a piece entitled *A System for a Repeating Exposition of a Composition for Sixteen Umbrella Position Possibilities;* or *Energy Transformation/Accumulation Device with (Time Program)/ (Energy Distribution/Umbrella Positioner) Apparatus* (1974). This work features a row of four open umbrellas, each of which is animated to move up and down via a pneumatic cylinder at the base of its shaft. A programmable timing device orchestrates the movement of the umbrellas and sets them up in sixteen of the possible positions within a one-minute cycle.

Easily, the most ambitious of all the umbrella works is also the most recent. After tabling the image for a number of years, Rogers was invited by the Portland Contemporary Crafts Gallery to create an installation to fill the entire facility which was celebrating its fiftieth year of operation in 1988. An enormous task, Rogers appropriately decided to comprise the exhibit of fifty umbrellas that were to be positioned throughout the floor, wall, and ceiling space of the galleries, while moving in a variety of fashions. The resulting work, entitled *Umbrellachron-CCG50,* featured umbrellas that spun, swayed, and dropped. The work was accompanied by a booming soundtrack of a thunderstorm.

The second major body of work by Rogers commenced in the mid-1970s. While in the Federal Republic of Germany on a year-long arts fellowship, Rogers began his first investigations into the concept of "time." Delving into this idea with the same fervor as demonstrated by the earlier umbrella pieces, he first made a series of static works that took the four letters from the word "time" and constructed a sculpture from these letters. Upon his return to the United States, Rogers began to investigate the kinetic possibilities of "time." Most notably from this series of investigations was the aforementioned fish-killing piece, *A Matter of Time.* Other "time" works included *Time of Your Life. Time of Your Life* was a two-passenger Ferris wheel. However, the two seating positions were a baby carriage and a wheelchair. The resulting meaning is self-evident.

As the decade came to an end, so did this series of "time" works. The main focus of Rogers's attention now began to swing towards his most monumental project to date. In an effort to create a work whose presence extended well beyond the typically regional outlets, Rogers conceived of the work entitled *Odyssetron.* The work would be executed gradually over a period of ten to twenty years. The piece would take place in four phases, with the final phase crystallizing in the creation of a "Cybernautical Metamodel"

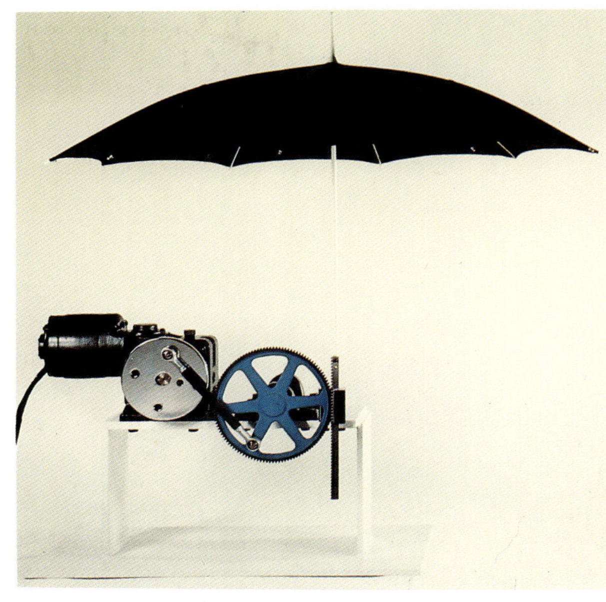

PHOTO BY BILL GHIORSO. COLLECTION DR. AUSTIN CONKEY, SAN FRANCISCO

Bryan Rogers, *Machine to Move an Umbrella Up and Down,* 1973. Umbrella, gear motor, mounting and motion linkage hardware. 41x36x35 inches. The umbrella moves up and down twelve times each minute.

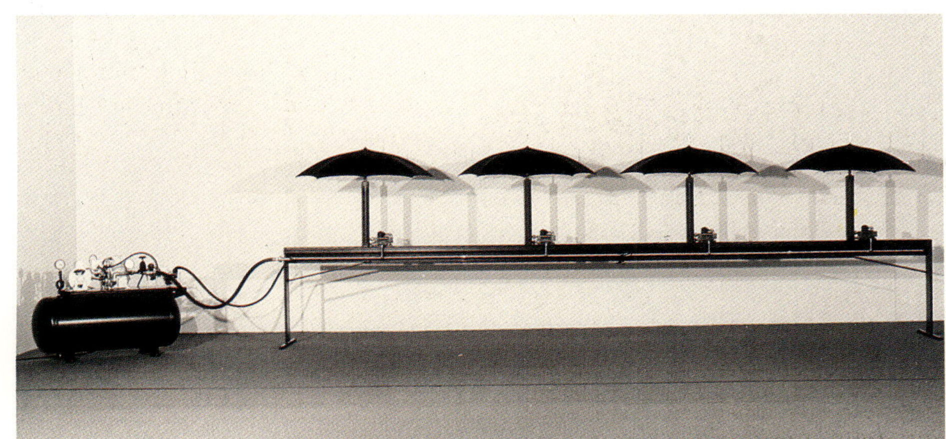

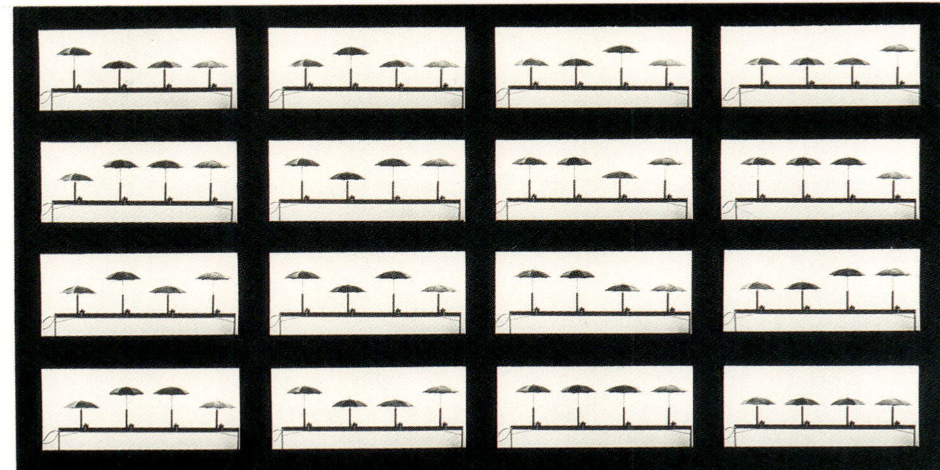

Bryan Rogers, *A System for Repeating Exposition of a Composition for Sixteen Umbrella Position Possibilities, or, Energy Transformation/Accumulation Device with (Time Program)/(EnergyDistribution/Umbrella Positioner) Apparatus,* 1974. Umbrellas, pneumatic cylinders, compressor, electromechanical timer, miscellaneous hardware. Periodically the set of four umbrellas is pneumatically activated to move up and down in a sequence which explores the sixteen up-and-down combinations, also shown here.

Bryan Rogers, *Umbrellachron—Model CCG50,* 1987.
Fifty umbrellas, motors, microprocessor-based timer, miscellaneous hardware.
A fifty-umbrella installation designed to utilize three interconnected gallery spaces. A timer is used to sequence and control the motion of the umbrellas in a twenty-minute program starting with the motion of individual umbrellas and then progressing to systems of similarly kinetic umbrellas and then to a complex finale with all fifty umbrellas in motion. Sounds of rain and thunder fill the gallery during the program.

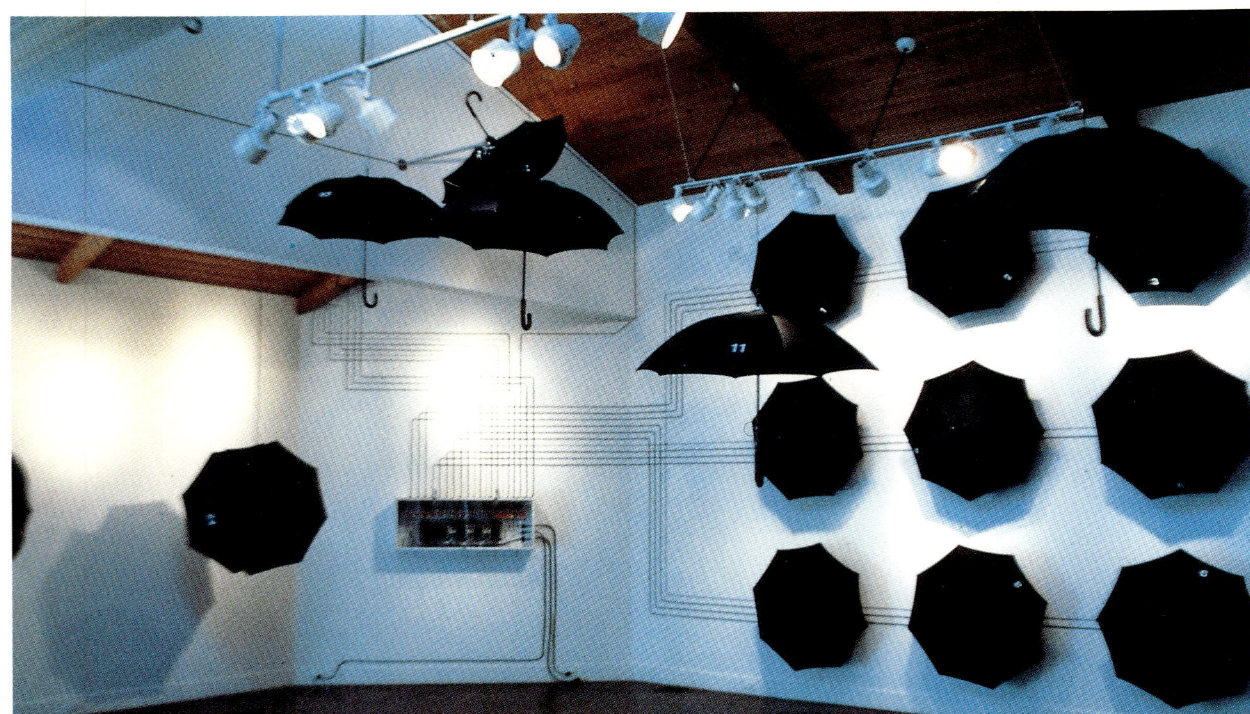

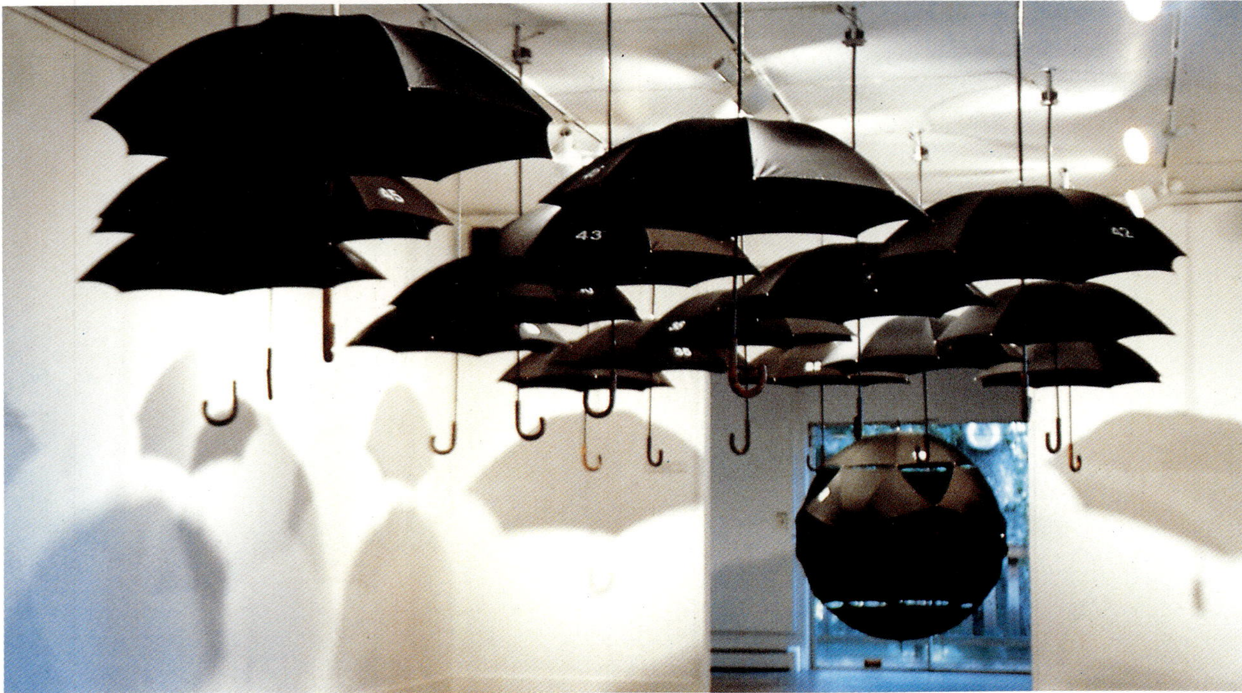

whose mission would be to circumnavigate the oceans of the earth.

Phase 1 was successfully executed in 1980. It consisted of the creation of 100 free-floating, anthropomorphic modules that were launched in the San Francisco Bay, as well as the surrounding waterways in the area. These modules contained information about the project graphically depicted on the outside of the piece. Having also included a post office box number to which the finder of these modules could report, to date Rogers has received word that over one third of the initial 100 have been found. This amount of response has far exceeded his expectations.

Following the completion of Phase 1, Rogers tabled the *Odyssetron* project to assume the role of editor for the sole publication dedicated to science and technology in the arts, the *Leonardo* journal. As homage to his friend, and founder of the journal, Frank Malina, Rogers took over production of the publication at the time of Malina's death in 1982. The all-consuming editorial responsibilities came to an end in 1985, coinciding with an invitation from the organizers of the 18th International Bienal of Sao Paulo to create an installation for their exhibit entitled *Between Science and Fiction.* The timing of the request was perfect for Rogers to move into Phase 2 of the *Odyssetron* project. For the exhibit, he displayed a series of lithographs describing the project, as well as a prototype for the Phase 2 module. As Phase 1 concerned itself with the two-dimensional display of information, Phase 2 involves the construction of sixty-four modules that will transmit information. Rogers is, at the time of this writing, in the process of fabricating these units. The launch site predicted for this series is to be the waters surrounding the Hawaiian Islands. These units will be solar powered and will transmit various patterns of electronic tones.

Phase 3 of the project will involve the launching of sixteen modules that are capable of both transmitting and receiving information. And finally, the aforementioned Phase 4 will involve the construction of one solar-powered, self-propelled unit that will be capable of circumnavigating the waterways of the world. Though the path of this unit will be monitored by Rogers, this module will be completely self-guided. If successful, this culmination will justify the initial concept of the project inspired by the journeys of Homer's Odysseus. As Odysseus traveled on global adventures, victimized by the throngs of the unknown, his ultimate guiding force was the homeward return.

UPPER LEFT PHOTO BY JOE SAMBERG

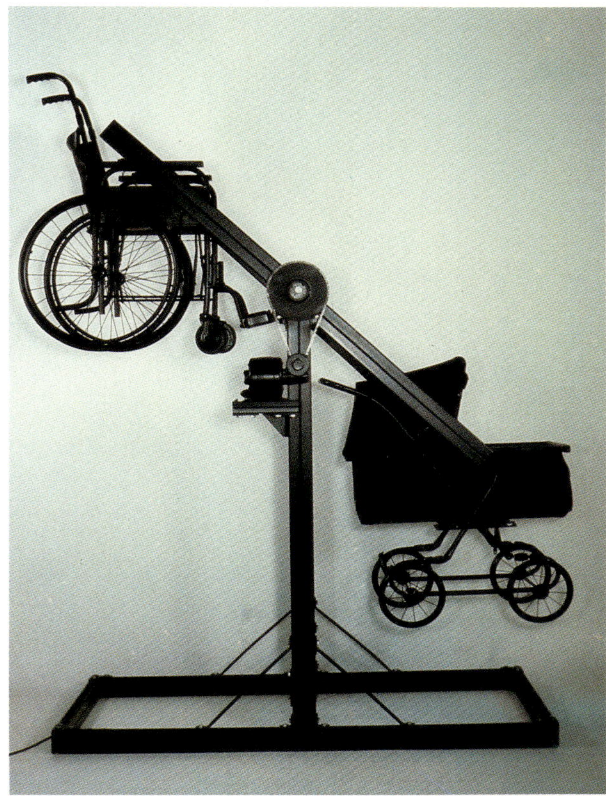

Bryan Rogers, *Time of Your Life,* 1978. Wheelchair, baby carriage, gear motor, hardware. 88x42x30 inches. The wheelchair/baby carriage structure revolves at a speed of twelve revolutions per minute.

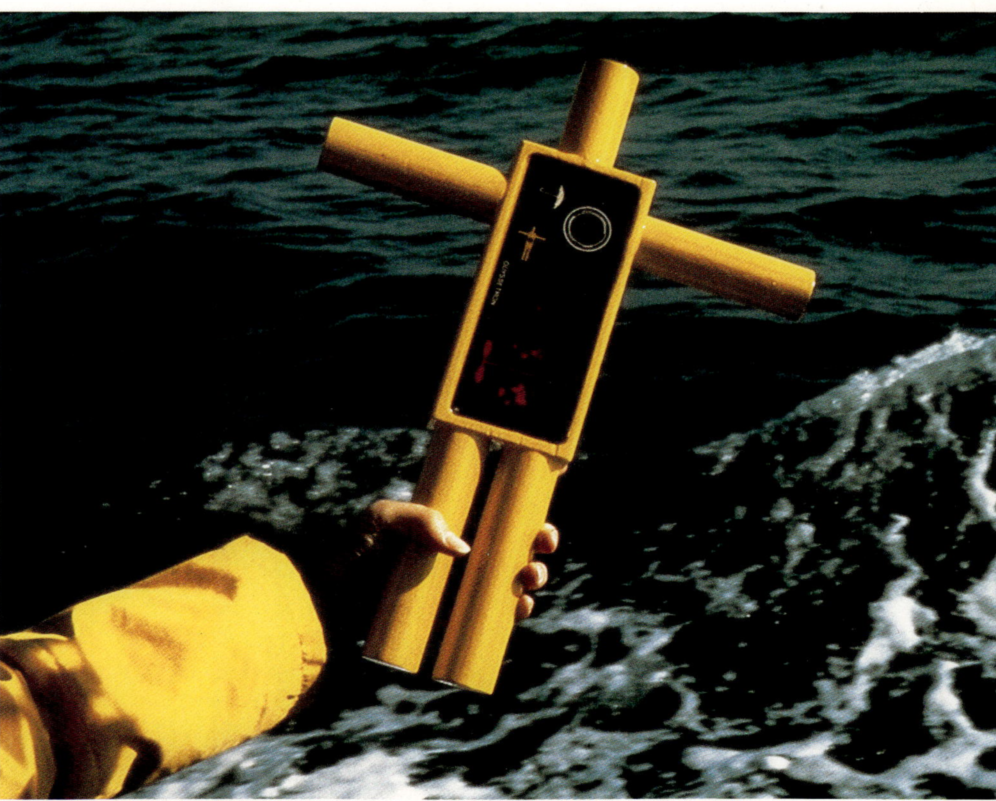

Bryan Rogers, *Odyssetron: A Cybernautical Metamodel,* Phase 1, 1980. One hundred Modules such as this one were launched in the San Francisco Bay water system in 1980.

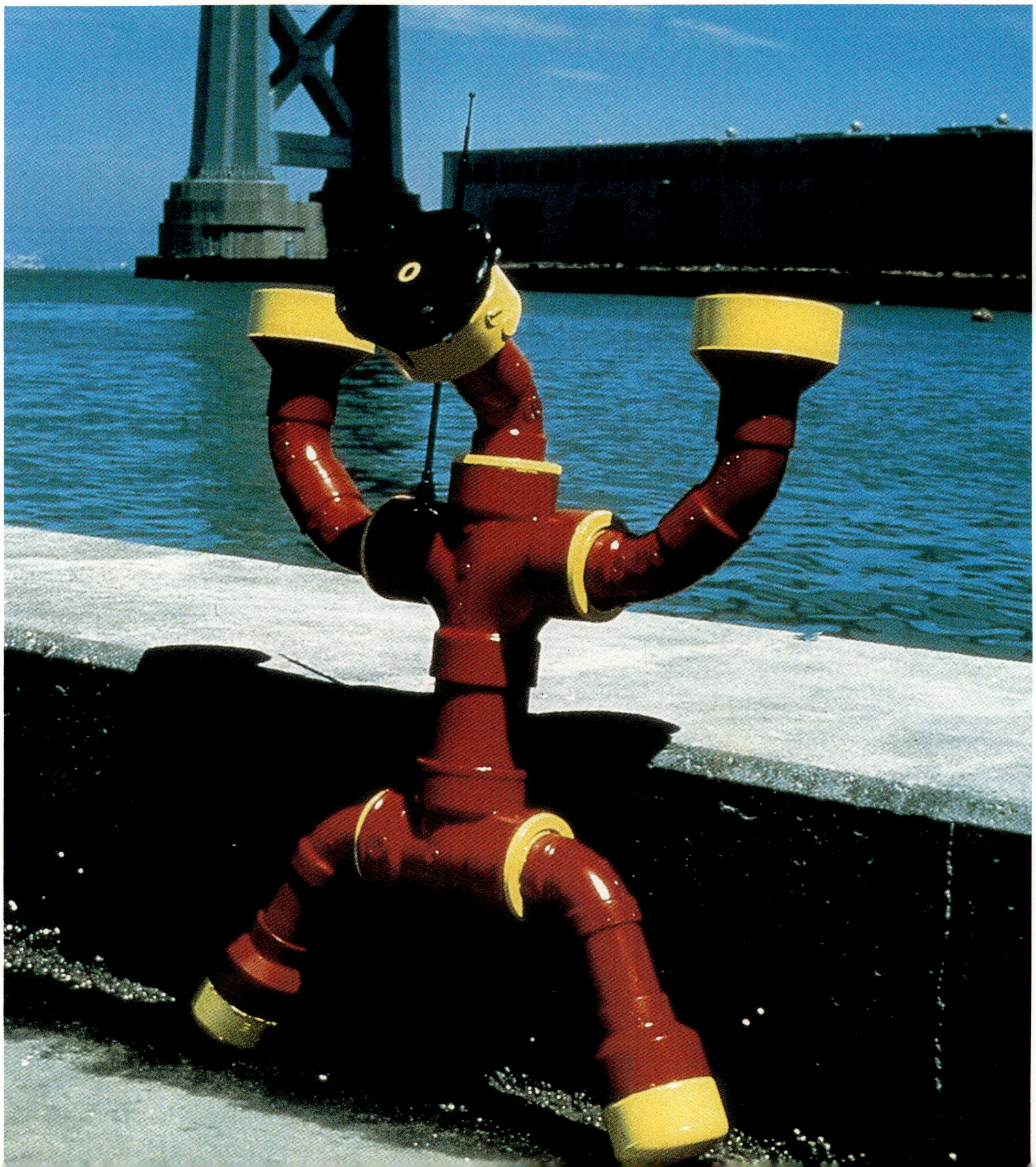

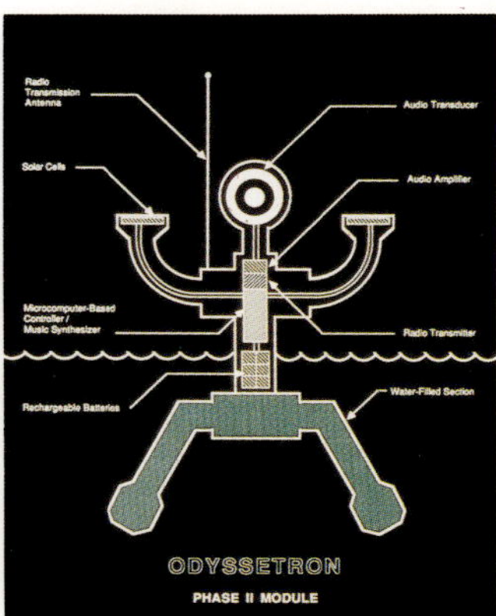

Bryan Rogers, *Odyssetron: A Cybernautical Metamodel,* Phase 2 prototype module and schematic diagram, 1980. A solar-powered microcomputer-based module containing a music synthesizer which periodically transmits music both acoustically and on a specified radio frequency.

Survival Research Laboratories

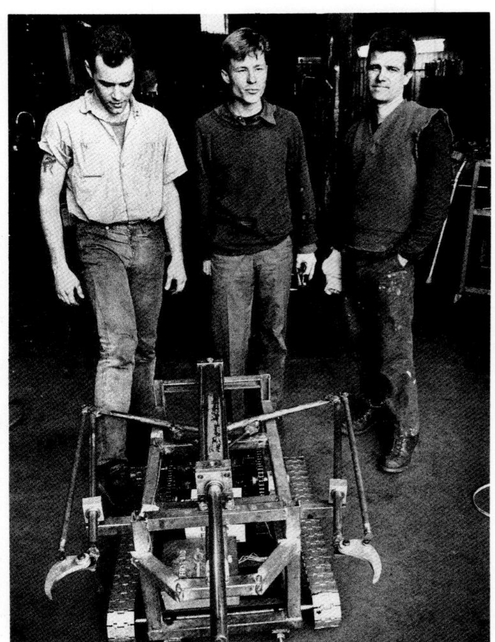

Left to right, Eric Werner, Matt Heckert, and Mark Pauline.

PHOTO BY ERICH MUELLER

FANTASTIC MACHINES IN FRENETIC performance bonded by a ruthless nihilism is the art trademark of the San Francisco triumvirate who call themselves Survival Research Laboratories (SRL). It is carnage spawned from industrial wreckage – SRL's palette is the Bay Area's rusting industrial legacy of World War II. SRL is arguably the aftermath of an awesome nationwide industrial mobilization that culminated in the successful nuking of Hiroshima and Nagasaki. Few other art efforts enjoy such eager attention, or spawn such heated controversy, as does SRL's mechanical mayhem performance orgies of machine and fire, animal parts, and risk.

In force since 1980, the group's first Southern California "performance" on 11 August 1985 provided a typical glimpse of the commotion. Two thousand-plus art aficionados gathered in a grimy industrial lot on the west bank of the Los Angeles River to witness *Extremely Cruel Practices: A Series of Events Designed to Instruct Those Interested in Policies that Correct or Punish.* True to the evening's title, SRL delivered the promised "cruelty" and "punishment" for the spectators, each of whom had to sign a waiver releasing the artists from legal liability should the performance go awry and cause personal injury.

Well past the scheduled 8:00 P.M. starting time, the crowd cheered as SRL personnel approached a menagerie of sleeping machines. Much like the fanfare of "gentlemen start your engines" at the Indy 500, the SRL crew began pulling cords and tripping switches to one by one fire up the sculptures. The bullring was doused in a loudly amplified soundtrack of abstracted body and industrial noises interspersed with occasional dialogue – "You say you were tortured?" a man would ask in clarity, the reply being an unintelligible woman's voice. Soon, the entire lot was crawling with all manner of pneumatics, hydraulics, and internal combustion. From the background rolled the one-ton *Tower of Power,* head spinning, arms flailing. An army of four limp-legged *Sneaky Soldiers* crawled by their arms in haphazard, hopeless circles. A spike-wheeled steamroller bumped across the lot. The ingenious *Screw Machine* – a pair of pneumatic arms and elaborate drive system mounted atop two rollered augers – molested the other machines under radio control of Mark Pauline.

Survival Research Laboratories, *Sneaky Soldier,* 1985. An army of four similar creations crawled about aimlessly in a famous 1985 outdoor performance.

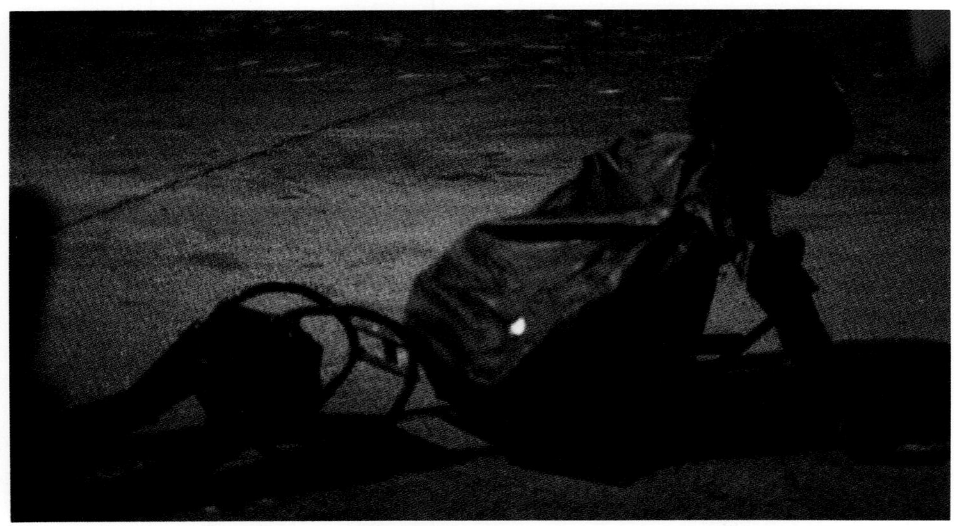

PHOTO BY DAVID FAMILIAN

Loosely orchestrated, a score of machines clashed in conflict. The *Screw Machine* tugged a plastic tarp, exposing the *Big Man,* a fire-breathing buzz saw wielding two-story tall human chassis. A mighty catapult lobbed fire bombs, igniting target machines and lighting the scene of battle. A loud gasoline-powered winch was started, engaged, and a pig carcass was ripped in half. A high-speed saw was slowly grinding a circle in asphalt, spraying a rooster tail of sparks. A "mechanized tusk" crept about the perimeter of the battlefield, slapping the *Sneaky Soldiers* and accosting other targets. As the battle wore on, the two visually dominant pieces – *Tower of Power* and *Big Man* – engaged in an epic duel. *Tower of Power* nunchucked *Big Man* who, in turn, spewed fire upon his adversary. In less than an hour the entire performance ground down – surviving sculptures were deactivated by SRL personnel, the lights dimmed, and the grating soundtrack quieted. The grand finale was signaled by the launching of marine emergency flares that drifted back to earth on miniature parachutes. Amid the smoking wreckage, the crowd cheered and in the quiet of the denouement a few spectators stepped forward to purchase machine remnants signed by the SRL artists.

Thus a Los Angeles performance was added to the resume of the Survival Research Laboratories, a successor to previous public events such as *The Unrestrained Use of Excessive Force* and *An Epidemic of Fear: The Relief of Mass Hysteria Through Expressions of Senseless Jungle Hate.* It was an evening of punk and press. The L.A. show received major media attention, consistent with SRL's previous coverage by the "NBC Nightly News," "P. M. Magazine," *New Look* magazine, the *New York Times,* television's "Ripley's Believe It or Not," and German Public Television. SRL even won a NEA grant to help finance their investigations of machine and performance.

It is possible to separate SRL's machines, the kinetic contrivances, from the larger performances in which they participate, insofar as several SRL works have appeared in more traditional gallery shows. A group exhibition "San Francisco/Science Fiction" (Otis/Parsons Art Gallery, April 1985) included Pauline's *Crawler,* a machine with an electric eye that reacts to its broken beam by spewing white fluid through a pair of false teeth. Also displayed was Heckert's *Jumping Machine* which torques a motor-

PHOTO BY DAVID FAMILIAN

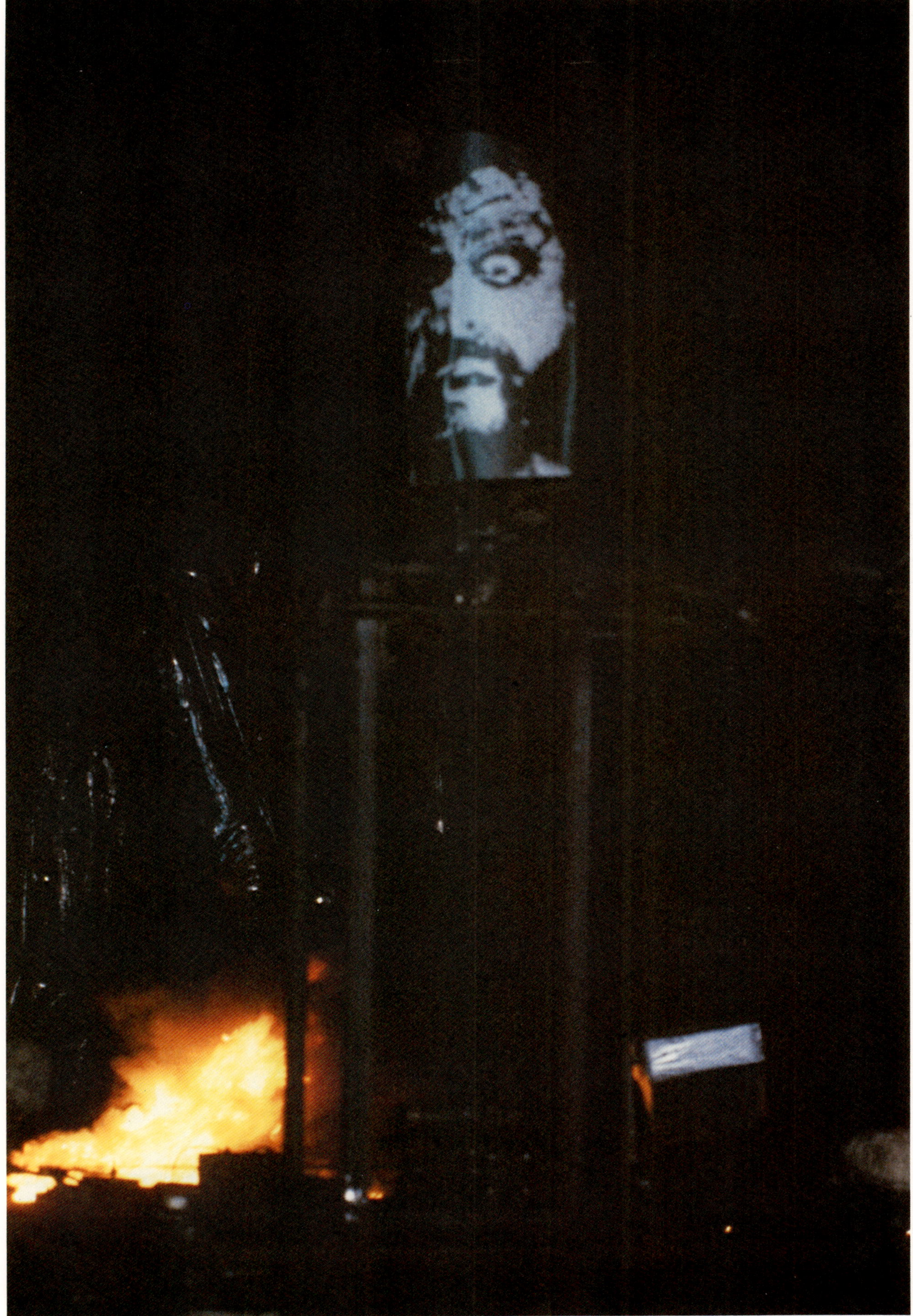

Survival Research Laboratories, *Tower of Power,* 1985.

cycle engine to cock itself and then spring upward, and Werner's *Mechanical Limb,* a menacing, surrogate hand and arm that emerges from an oil-filled aquarium, flexes itself, and sinks back into the ooze. (Werner built *Mechanical Limb* shortly after Pauline blew off most of his right hand experimenting with rocket fuel in 1982).

Even in the more traditional Otis/Parsons Art Gallery environment, the magnificent engineering and construction of SRL sculpture is subservient to its ominous, hostile, even nihilistic character. Indeed, violating art's axiom to treat all critics with kindness, Pauline's *Crawler* threw up its milky white stuff on *Los Angeles Times* art critic William Wilson, who panned "San Francisco/Science Fiction" for allegedly unrelated reasons.

States Pauline about SRL's mission: "We're trying consistently and consciously to create a different kind of image. We're trying to deal in a commerce of ideas, and we're doing it ruthlessly."

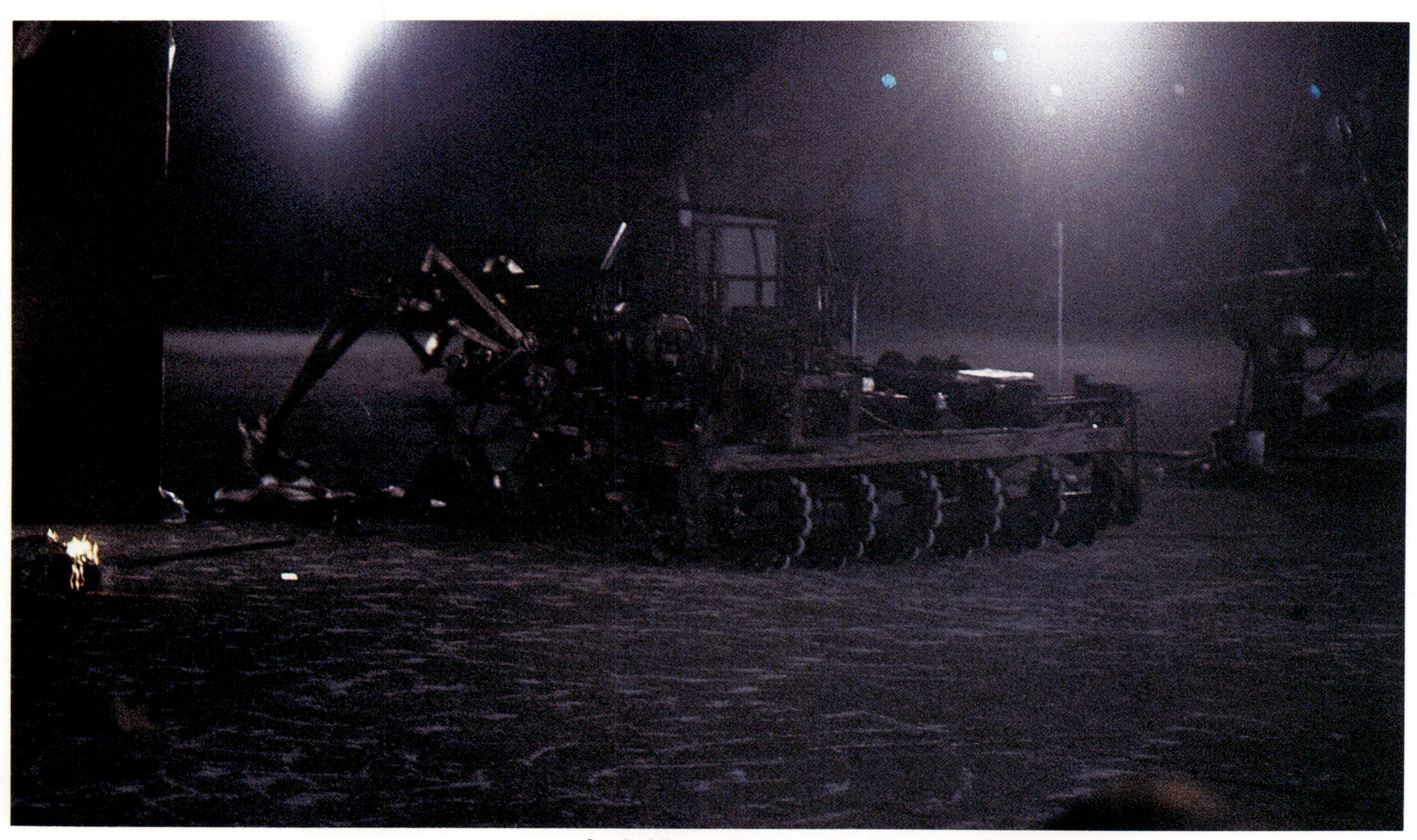

PHOTOS BY DAVE FAMILIAN

Survival Research Laboratories, *Clawed Screw Machine,* 1985.

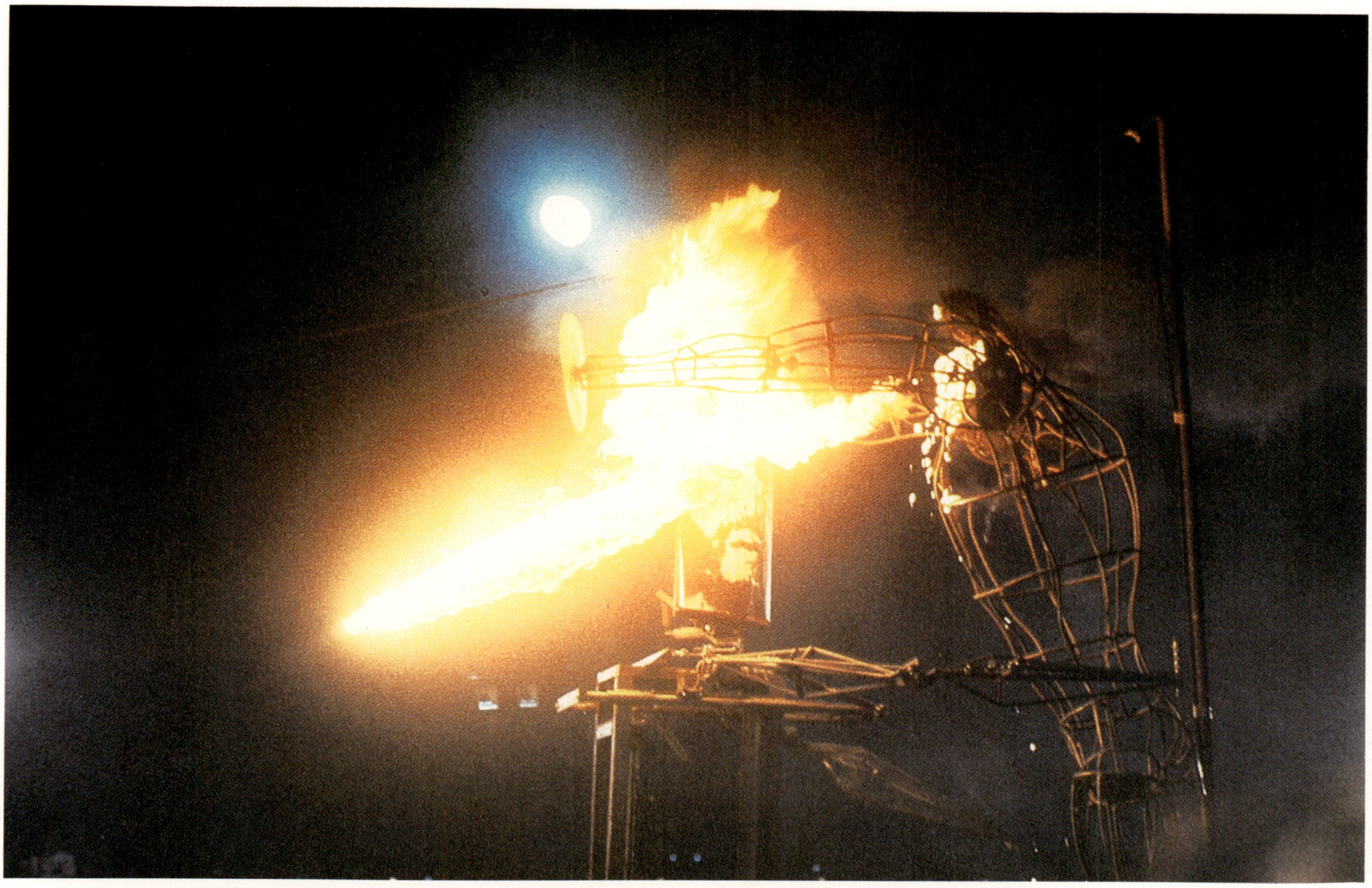

Survival Research Laboratories, *Big Man* fights *Tower of Power* in the group's 1985 performance *Extremely Cruel Practices: A Series of Events Designed to Instruct Those Interested in Policies That Correct or Punish.*

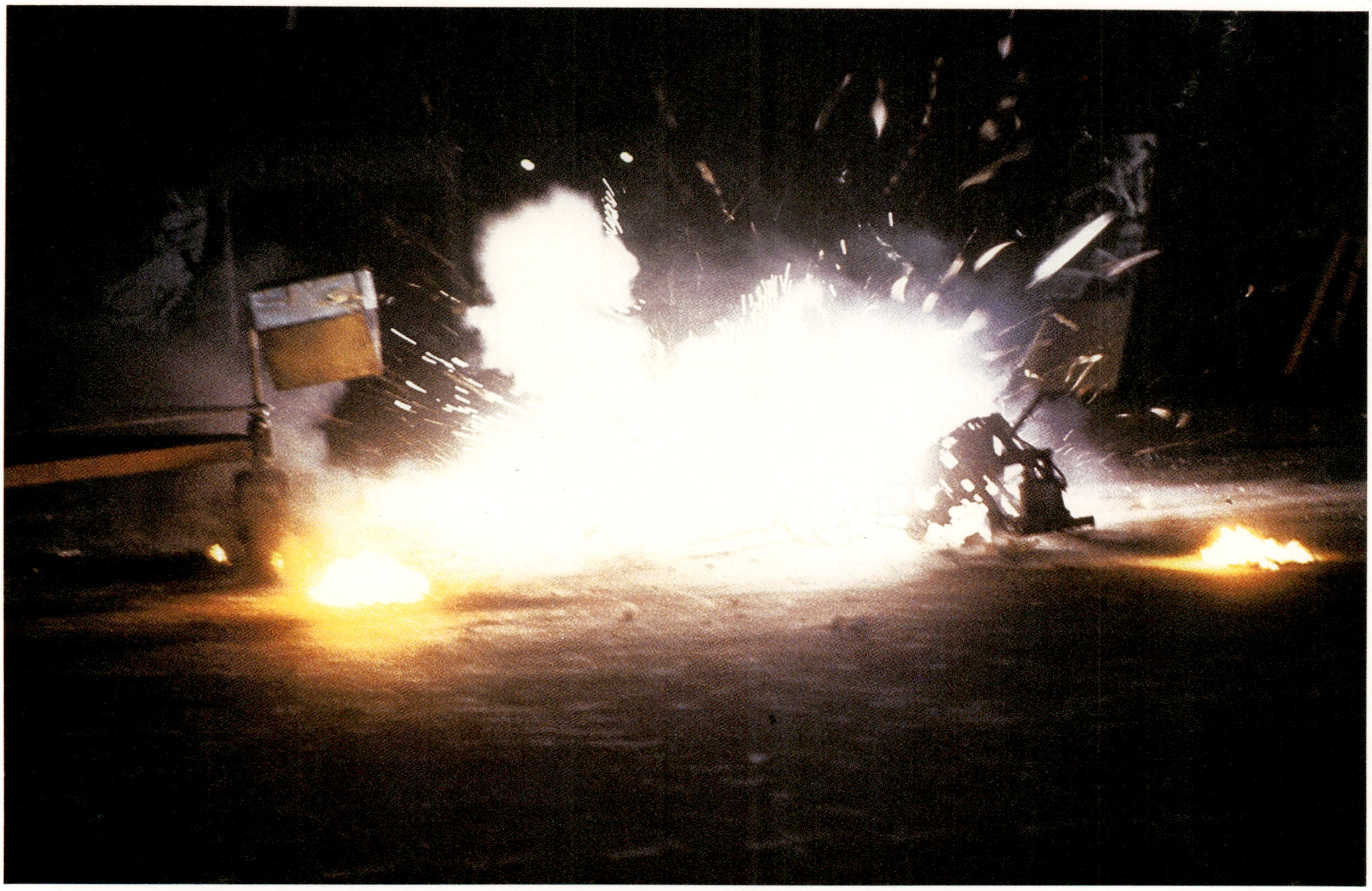

The hour-long 1985 Southern California performance was accompanied by an electronic soundtrack and included fire-spewing sculptures and the shredding of animal carcasses.

Sarah Tamor

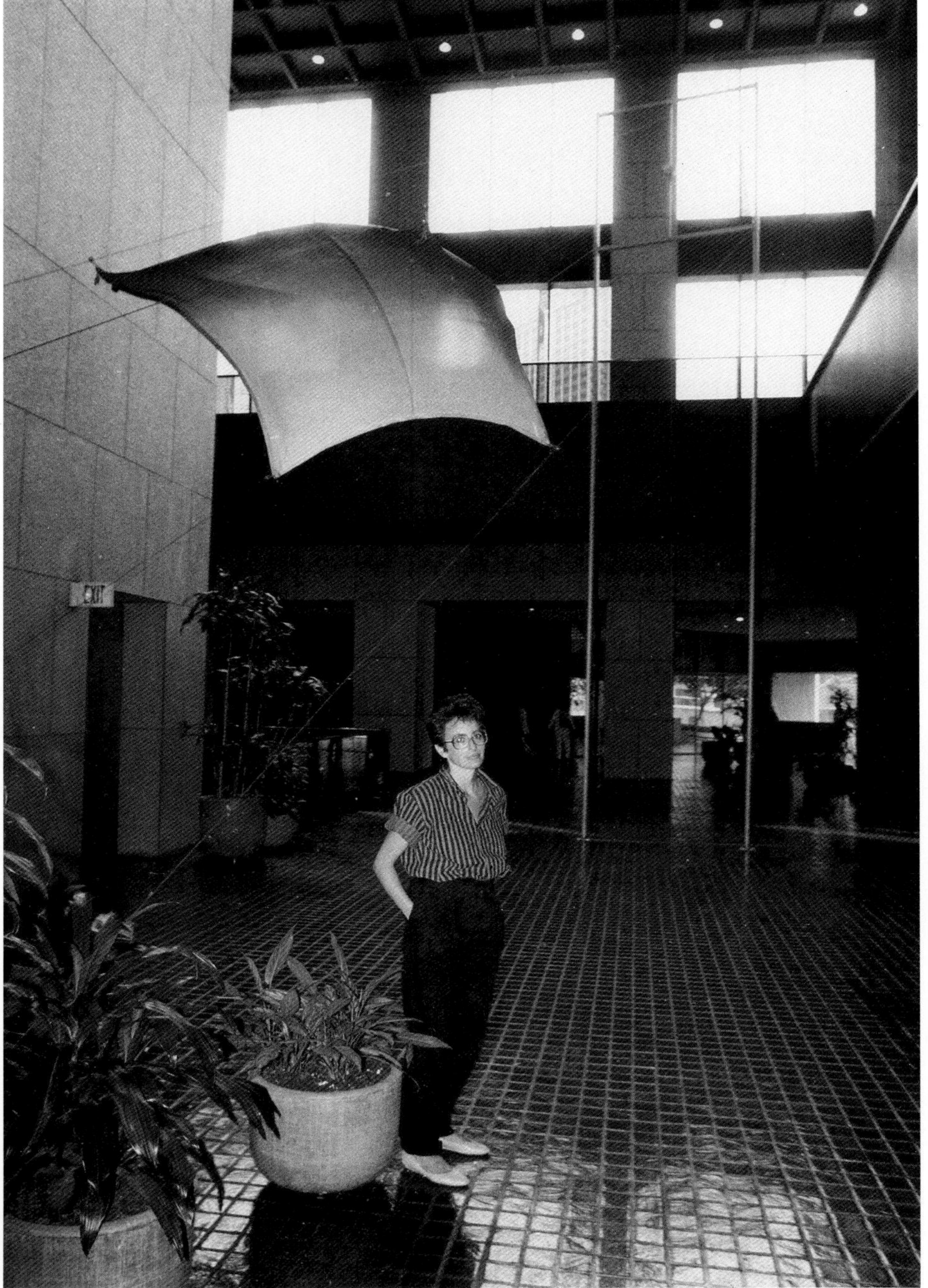

Sarah Tamor with her three-story tall *Bird for Angelou*, 1983–85.
Silk, aluminum tubing, cable, motor. 30x6x100 feet.

SINCE 1983 VISITORS TO THE CAVERNOUS LOBBY OF Security Pacific Bank's downtown Los Angeles high-rise headquarters have been greeted by Sarah Tamor's three-story tall *Bird for Angelou.* Running twenty-four hours a day, Tamor's landmark installation gently tugs a six-foot-square pink pastel silk panel upward; as it nears the top of the assembly the panel is released and it parachutes downward in a fifty-foot free fall. The flowing movement of the fabric defines and visualizes invisible forces that Tamor seeks to delineate. With this economical structure, the artist has created a monumental sculpture of substantial dimension and virtually no mass. Her employment of random movement activates dead space in the giant lobby's ceiling area and argues against the architect's hard angular design.

According to the artist, "The scale of *Bird for Angelou* was an attempt to activate the space without actually enveloping the viewer. The largeness of the work allows an adequate presence, without being overwhelmed."

Monumental scale is a trademark of Tamor's moving sculpture. Her first such major installation in a public place was *Flights Against the Grid* which was installed in the San Jose State University Student Union Building in 1981. The Student Union (the Grid) presents a structured architectural design – including three interior stairwells each five stories high. For the occupant standing on the ground floor, all three stairwells are visible.

Within each stairwell Tamor installed a cable and winch assembly that enabled viewers to crank a piece of fabric five stories high, or release the fabric into free fall at any point along its upward path. The graphic images of a rectangle and a curve were sewn into each sheet – "the rectangle relating to the space itself and curve relating to the motion of the fabric," states Tamor. The three assemblies operated independently, thus resulting in a sporadic, random relationship within the larger building space.

Flights Against the Grid was "an attempt to soften the space," says Tamor. The harsh, high-tech lines of the building were mitigated by the random rise and fall of three independently operated sculptures. A larger question is one of control – the building's precise design and strict "grid" presents Man in complete control of his environment. Tamor's installation presented the opposite to the viewer, who could only control one third of the assembly at any one time with the remaining two thirds in control of others.

Tamor's next major installation, her first outdoors, abandoned mechanical winch motion in favor of the natural force of the wind. *Echo Park* was installed at the head of a ravine in a wooded hillside near downtown Los Angeles. Towering upwards seventy feet into eucalyptus treetops, *Echo Park*'s four lines of cable supported a rectangle of ripstop nylon. The horizontal flag played up and down the cables, propelled by the ravine's capricious wind currents. Tamor observed, "The wind-driven aspect of *Echo Park* allowed the fabric to have a much wider vocabulary of motion than a mechanism offered. The work also deals with the articulation of the unseen forces of wind and gravity." To a degree, the installation sought to incorporate nature within its natural setting – yet still represented human intrusion by mechanical structure.

Subsequent to her fabric-in-motion installations, Tamor has been seeking additional materials that would "allow flexibility as opposed to the rigidity of steel or wood." Wire mesh seemed to be such a material. The variety of screen texture and pattern available has allowed her to play with aspects of both transparency and heaviness. Utilizing the so-called "moire effect" by layering screens and creating opti-

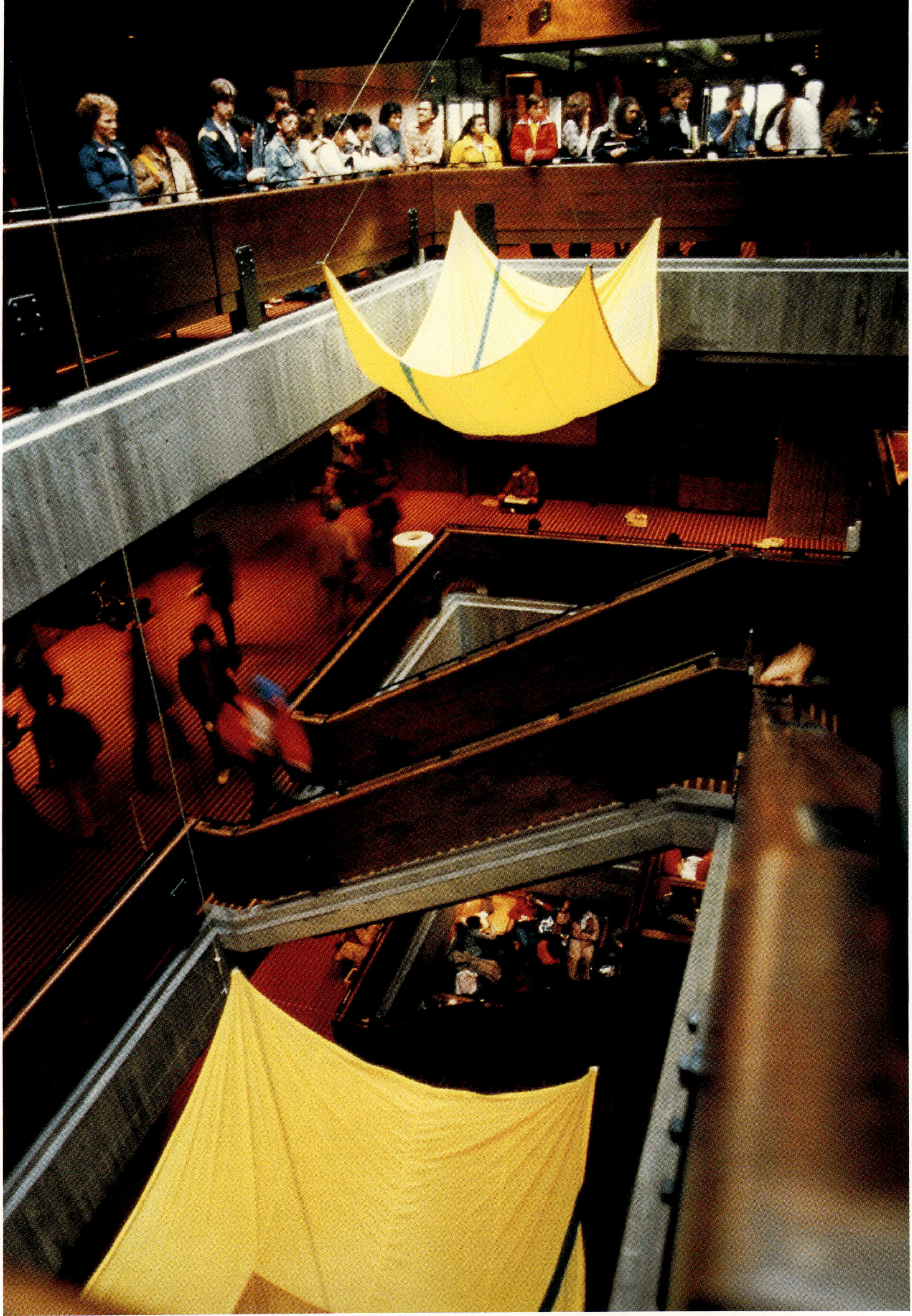

Sarah Tamor, *Flights Against the Grid,* 1981. Ripstop nylon, cable, winch. 50x42x15 feet. A cable and winch system allows viewers to crank a piece of fabric up to five stories into the air, releasing it to free fall to the bottom of the stairwell.

cal interaction between the patterns, Tamor has effectively substituted the physical motion of her previous works for "optical motion" which is achieved as the viewer, not the art, moves within the space.

Tamor thus retains her fundamental interest in space altered by movement. A constant of Tamor's monumental installations is their incorporation of motion to establish contrast, even conflict, against their environments. Among the precise lines of high-rise architecture, Tamor violates order with randomness. In the natural environment of hillside eucalyptus, she imposes order and human machinery, though never on a permanent basis. Even the strictly ordered mesh pattern of screen grids can be violated, made illusionary, by Tamor's use of motion.

Tamor observes, "There's always contrasts going on in my work; up-down, hard-soft, large-small. I'm a twin and I think it all sort of comes back from defining myself always in opposition to something, to somebody else."

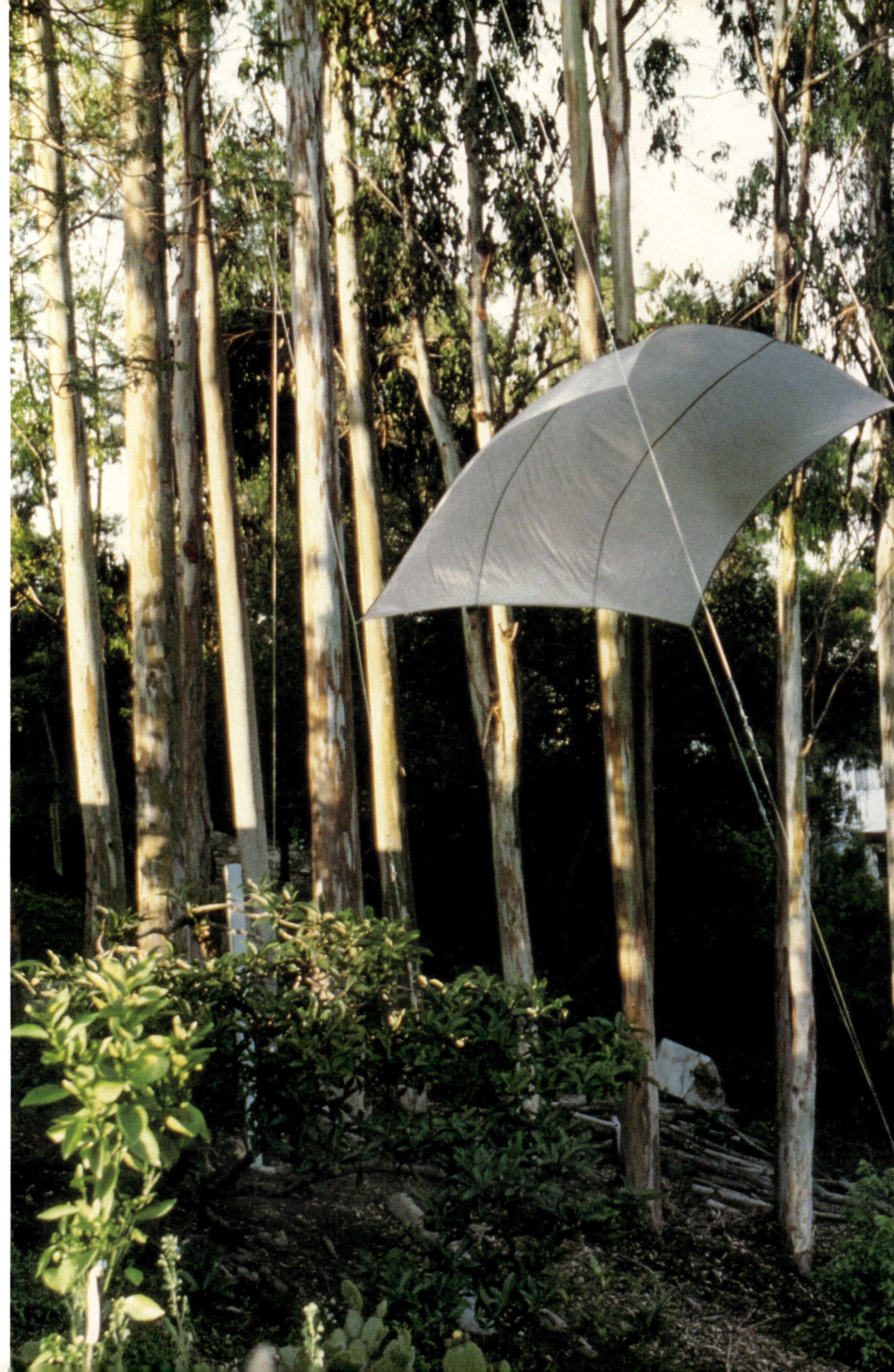

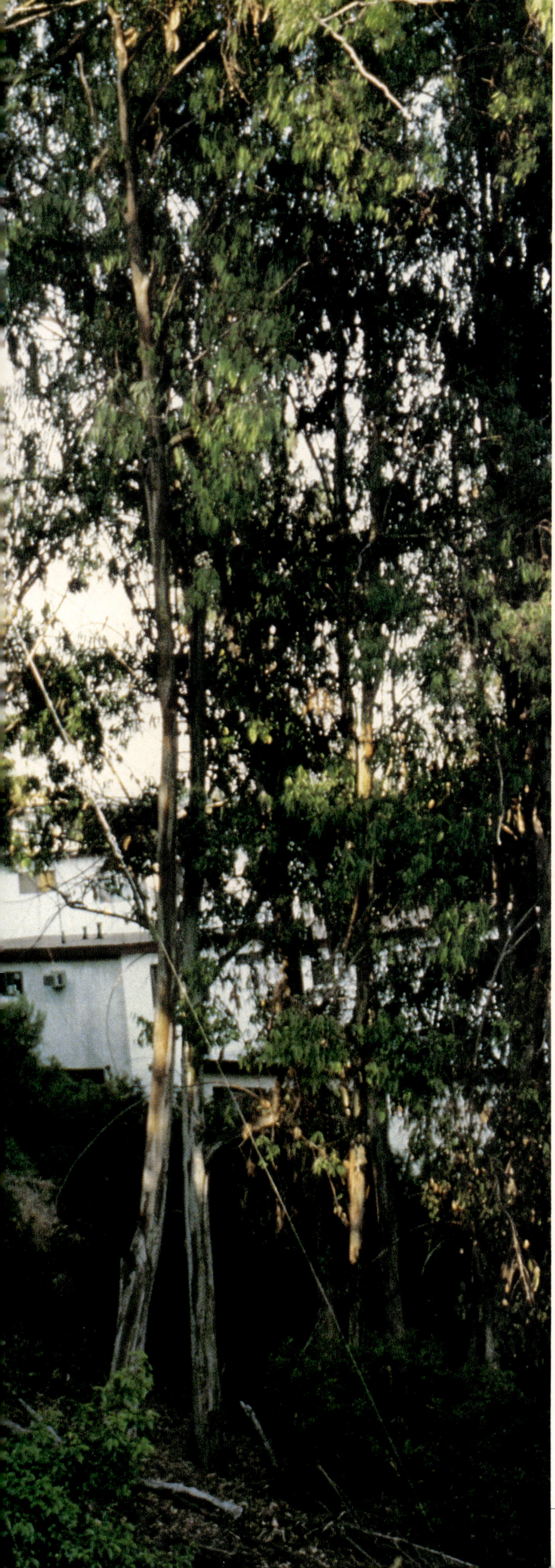

Sarah Tamor, *Echo Park,* 1982. Ripstop nylon, cable, PVC tubing. In Tamor's first outdoor installation, a horizontal piece of fabric plays up and down the cables, propelled by the everchanging wind currents of a ravine near downtown Los Angeles.

Fred Tomaselli

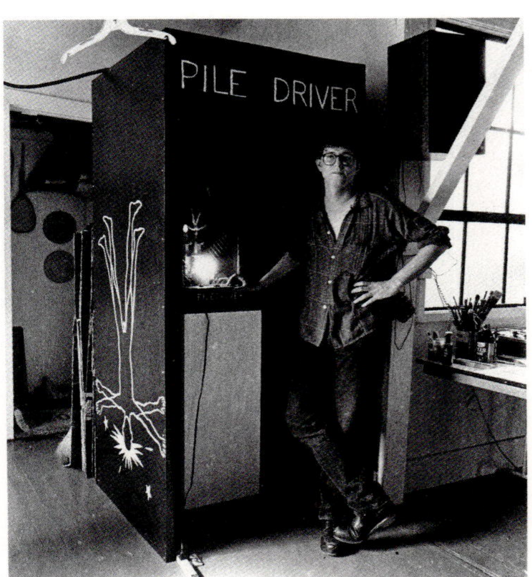

Fred Tomaselli, with his 1984 sculpture *Pile Driver.*

FRED TOMASELLI BUILDS STREET art. Both in topic and materials, his first found-object kinetic assemblages were constructed from the seedy avenues of Los Angeles's aged downtown industrial district where he had a studio. It is a landscape of bizarre contrasts populated at day by professionals in Porsches, and at night by a roaming army of homeless indigents from whom industrialism and technology have yielded zero dividends.

Nerve Twitch Leg Bottom and *The Rocker* hauntingly depict Tomaselli's derelict neighbors. The *Nerve Twitch* legs lurch when the viewer steps on a hidden floor switch and activates a solenoid – a kinetic effect not unlike that of a heart attack victim jolting during defibrillation. *Nerve Twitch* is a movable assembly designed for installation in any downtown doorway that offers shelter for the night. *The Rocker* contains the suggestion of an upper torso lying face down on the pavement. The protohuman form rocks erratically, suggesting a derelict in seizure.

The electromechanics of Tomaselli's works are crude, low tech, "the hokeyness of real limited technology," in the words of the artist. "Want to see my equipment? I use a jigsaw and a power drill. If I can't cut it and can't drill it, then I can't use it." Machinery and electronic wizardry are secondary to Tomaselli's work. Rather, the artist incorporates machine-as-found-object into a larger statement of the human condition. Some element of human form can be found in virtually all Tomaselli assemblages.

Pile Driver features a video game format. The viewer steps inside an isolated booth in the rear of which stands a dimly lit glass-fronted box that offers a series of three switches labeled "Power," "Start," and "Speed (Death/Migraine)." Behind the glass stands a small rubber doll-man positioned on his head atop a mechanized plunger. Push a button, and both the doll-man and viewer are assaulted by cacophonous electromechanical noises and bright lights while the doll-man furiously thrashes about. The viewer, who initiated the tirade, is less a sadist and more a mutual victim of *Pile Driver*'s assault.

In *Swimmer,* two human silhouettes stroke through an imaginary sea of blue-green light. The swimmer at the rear of the installation is larger that life, and the second appears in a TV set in the foreground. Blowing air causes a plethora of styrofoam cups to sway in wave motion on the floor between the two swimming images. The viewer is seduced into attempting to correlate the two moving forms – an impossible task. *Swimmer* documents the inherent intrusion the electronic mass media imposes between subject and viewer.

Dancing Eyes audibly elevates two ping-pong eyeballs over bare speakers which emit an amplified hum. Sound waves cause the eyeballs to hover in constant motion. The piece is scaled to the human head, electronics hang like guts, and *Dancing Eyes* is an obvious metaphor of sound-induced insanity.

Trained academically as a painter, Tomaselli's transition to kinetic sculptor accompanied his move from California's conservative, suburban Orange County ("home of Disneyland") to the radical inner-city environment of downtown Los Angeles. Confronted, Tomaselli groped for a relevant artistic language:

> *"Painting has really lost a lot of its emotive power and it may be a bankrupt language. I still see paintings that really excite me, and I see static sculpture that really excites me, and I do my own static work. But the static language of expression that I was involved in [painting] seemed to be reduced by history to a kind of decorative motif, and it didn't have much to do with expression at all."*
>
> *"I was an auto mechanic for five years. I custom built bicycles. I've done plumbing, drywall construction, tinkering around, fixing things. But there was always a separation between that and my art, painting and drawing. It wasn't like I was integrating my whole being. That is what my art ought to be about. It is just finding out what you're about and just doing it."*

Tomaselli now lives in New York City, where he continues to scour the inner-city environment for the machines and images of his kinetic language, sculpture indigenous to the "downtown art movement" of recent years. Tomaselli observed, "I'm not so sure about the immediate staying power of this art form over the course of time. Time will only tell. But for right now it seems real relevant."

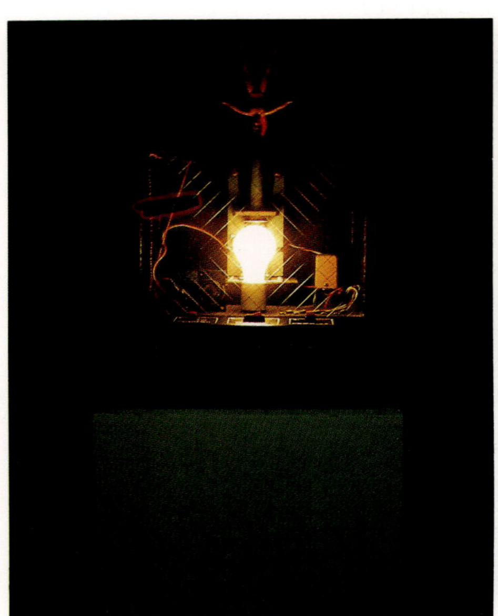

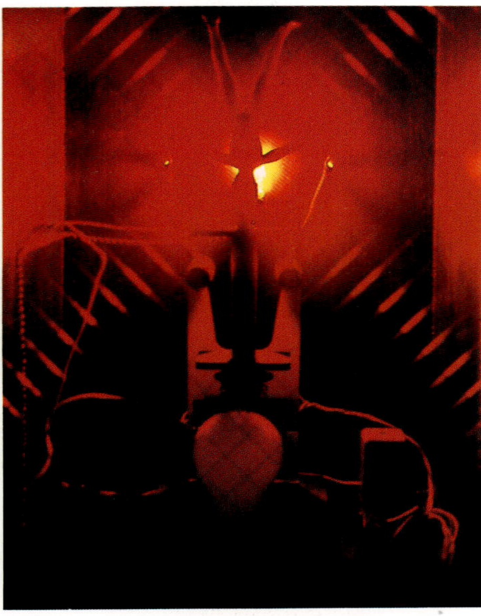

Fred Tomaselli, *Pile Driver,* 1984. Mixed media. 25x14x15 inches. A small rubber doll is subjected to a sensory and electronic assault at the hands of the viewer.

PHOTO BY ED GLENDINNING

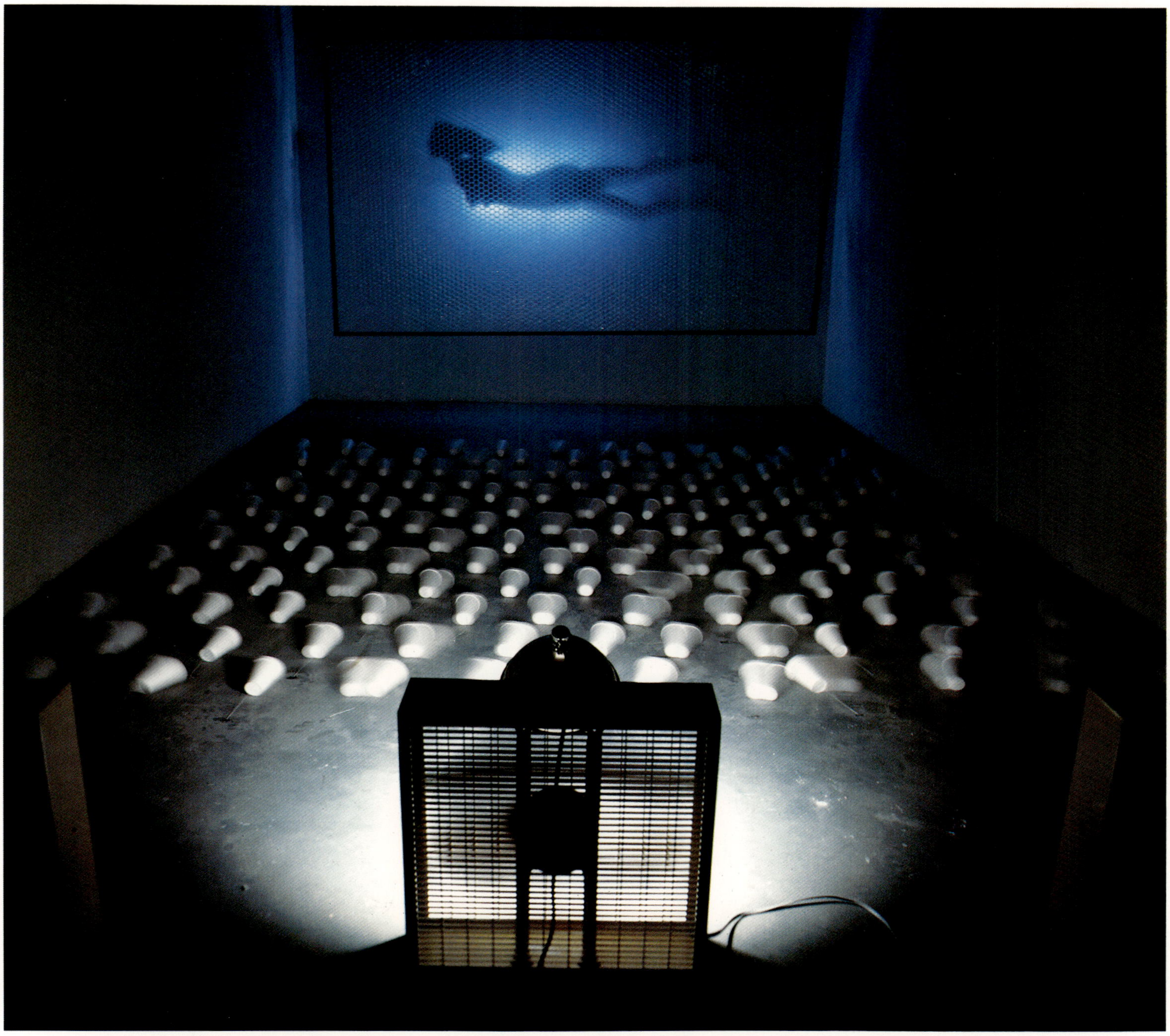

Fred Tomaselli, ***Shoreline,*** 1984. Mixed media. 13x40x13 feet. A larger-than-life swimmer strokes through an imaginary sea on the back wall while a floor fan causes the styrofoam cups on the floor to sway like ocean waves.

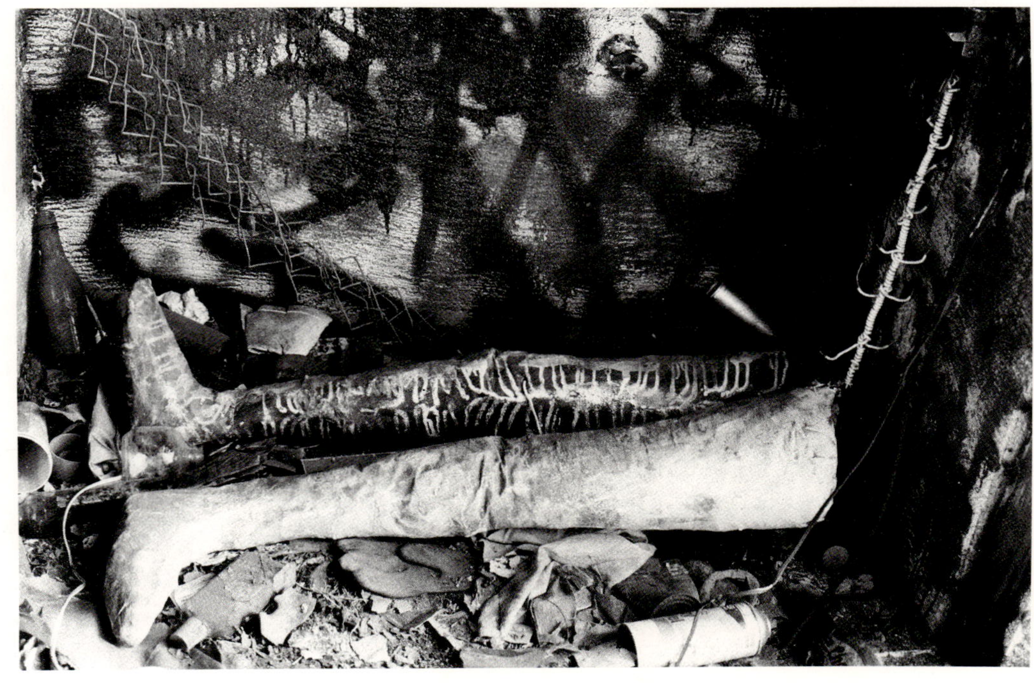

Fred Tomaselli, ***Nerve Twitch Leg Bottom,*** 1984. Mixed media. 3x5x8 feet. When the viewer steps on a hidden floor switch the legs lurch and twitch.

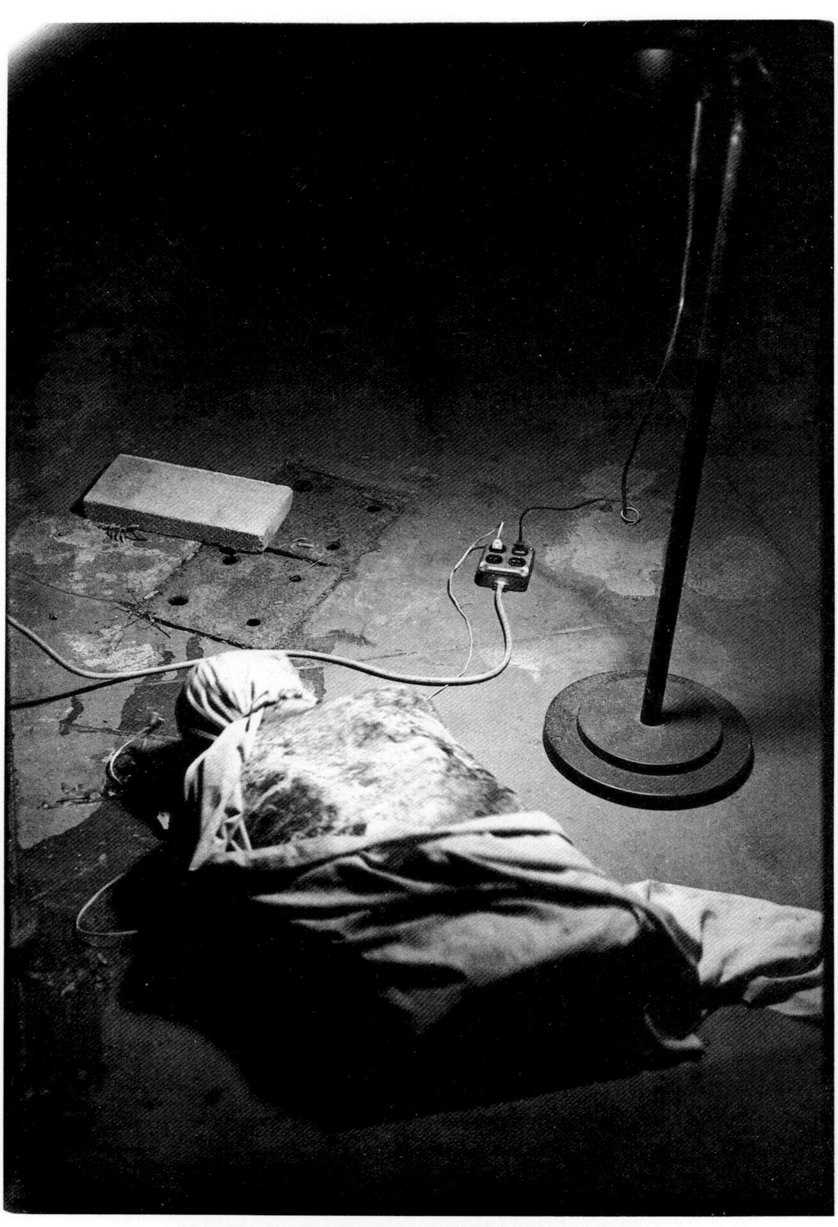

Fred Tomaselli, ***The Rocker,*** **1984. Mixed media.
48x20x11 inches. A torso lies face down on the pavement and rocks erratically as if having a seizure.**

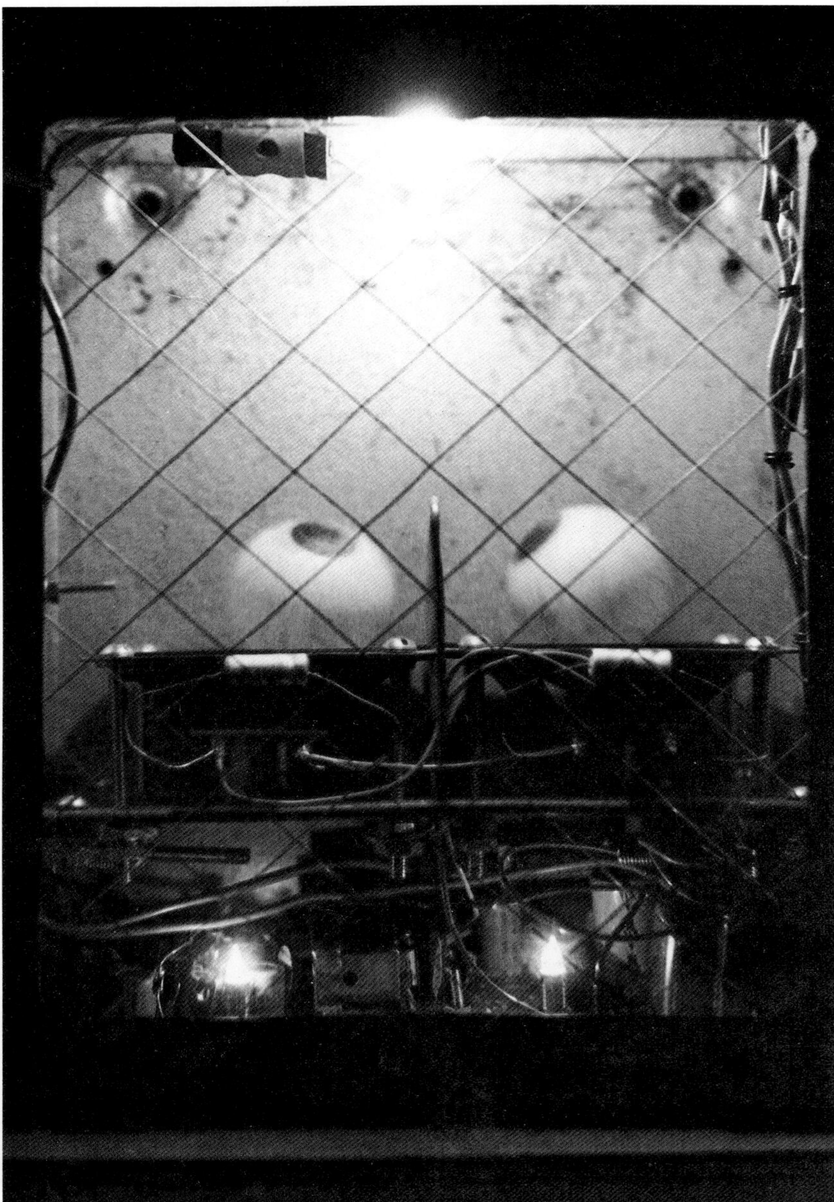

Fred Tomaselli, ***Dancing Eyes,*** **1985. Mixed media.
4x7x10 inches. Painted ping-pong balls hover suspended by sound waves over speakers which emit an amplified hum.**

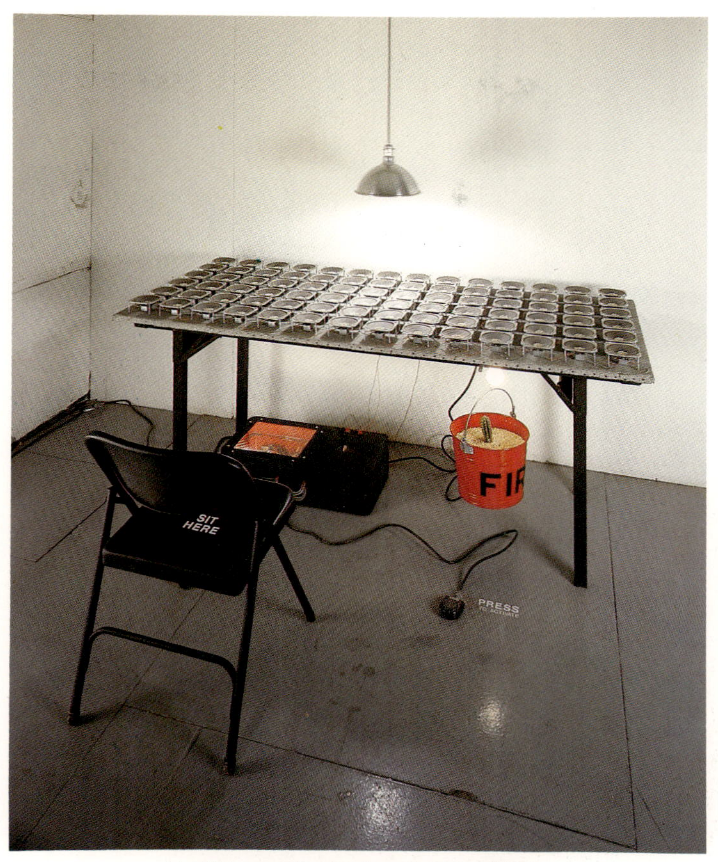

Fred Tomaselli, *Geology Lesson,* 1986.
Eighty-four speakers, cat litter, suitcase with electrical components. 30x72x32 inches. This viewer-activated work features the amplified hum of alternating current.

PHOTOS BY KEN SCHLES

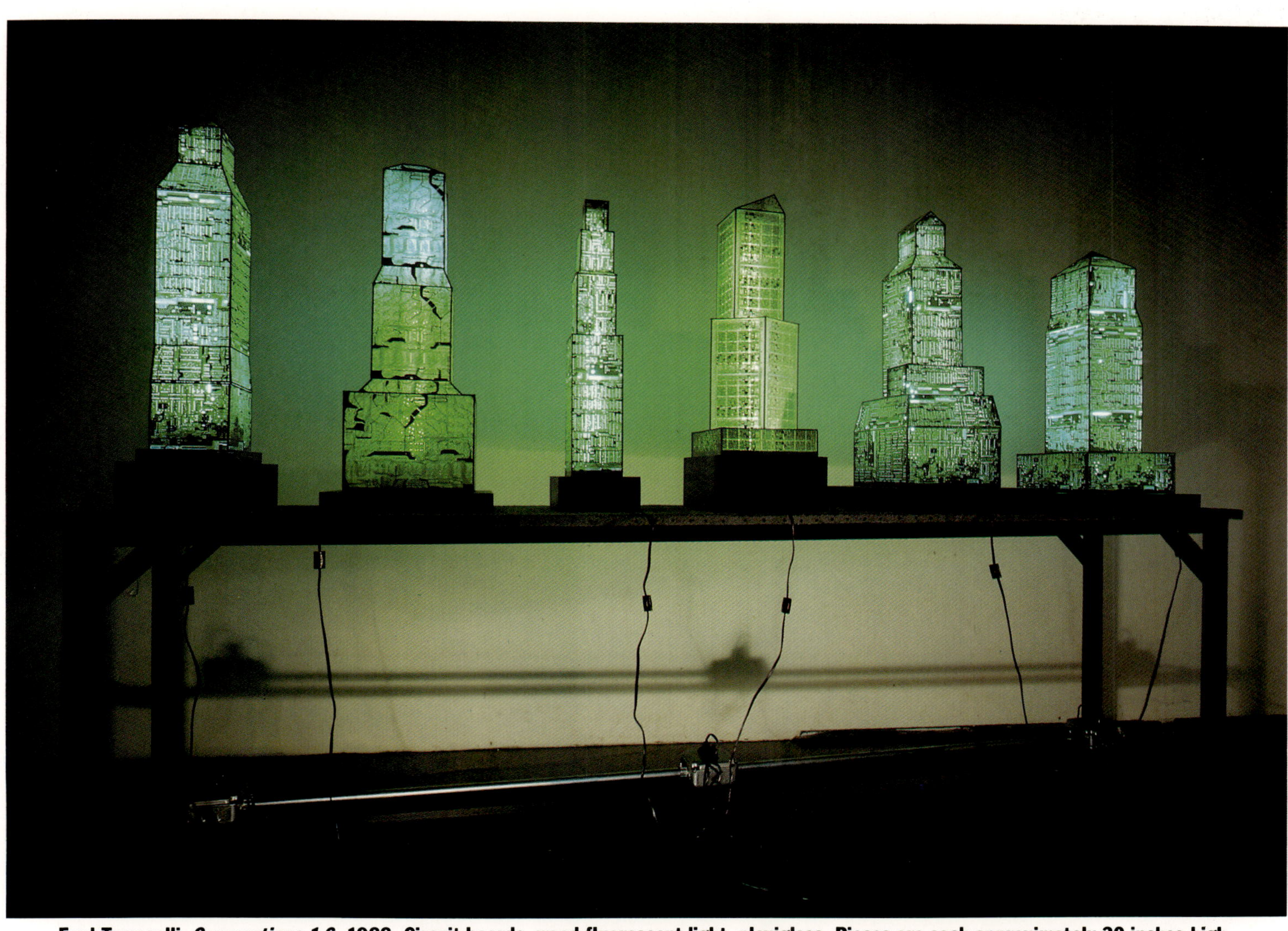

Fred Tomaselli, *Corporations 1-6,* 1988. Circuit boards, wood fluorescent light, plexiglass. Pieces are each approximately 30 inches high and sit on a table 30x96x18 inches. This series addresses the idea of technology rather than directly utilizing it. When the buildings (built out of printed circuit boards) are illuminated they are "working," or consuming power. When they are turned off they are "resting." The circuitry of the boards emulate the water and power systems of the buildings and the drilled out component holes suggest windows. Tomaselli sets up a metaphoric relationship between art, real estate, and technology since all are linked in the creation of wealth, as he sees it.

Steve Barry

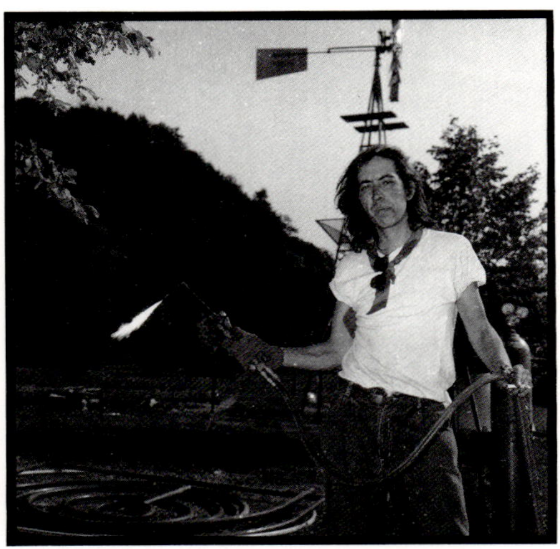

PHOTO BY HUGH CRAWFORD

IN 1964 STEVE BARRY'S PARENTS took him to the Vatican Exhibit at the New York World's Fair. Barry recalls in vivid detail the awesome imagery he witnessed from a moving sidewalk as it passed a replica of Michelangelo's *Pieta,* dimly shrouded in blue light. This experience thrilled the eight-year-old boy, not because of his rapture for art, but because of the surreal atmosphere within which he viewed the *Pieta.* The portable walkway, coupled with the space-age lighting, cast an illusion of undulation to the surface of the statue and etched a lasting impression on his young mind.

Fast forward some twenty years and one still finds Barry preoccupied with the qualities of motion and light. Barry builds "precinematic devices" – surrogate movie projectors – that explore the potential of moving images when placed in a sculptural context. Barry's "mechanical performances" contain narratives derived from Homeric mythology. These works are designed to engage the viewer in such a way that the proper operation of the sculpture actually depends upon the viewer's physical participation. Viewer involvement varies from piece to piece. It might be as slight as the person activating an "on" switch by sitting down before the sculpture, or as demanding as the work entitled *Xanthos* (1985).

In *Xanthos,* the viewer actually has to work to generate the image in a direct reference to turn-of-the-century nickelodeons. Instead of a hand crank, the piece features a treadmill upon which a person must walk. The motion of the revolving treadmill is transferred through the chassis to start up a projection unit. The image of a horizontally spinning figure is then directed back toward the viewer/walker onto a screen next to a shallow Plexiglas aquarium – the figure appears caught in a body of water. Occasional bubbles rise within the tank to heighten the illusion. The faster the viewer turns the treadmill, the faster the corpse in the river revolves.

The symbolism of *Xanthos* is derived from the Homeric myth about the River Xanthos (from the *Iliad*). The myth tells of Achilles's dumping slain Trojan soldiers into the river. Enraged by this action, Xanthos rose up from its banks in a futile attempt to drown Achilles.

Steve Barry, *Xanthos,* 1985. Steel, plastics, water, projector, film, strobe. 84x180x72 inches. A viewer-activated treadmill runs a projection unit which displays the image of a horizontally rotating figure. This motion picture is projected onto a bubbling aquarium positioned in front of the viewer.

PHOTO BY STEVE BARRY

Polythemus (1987), a large one-eyed sculpture, demands a bit more subtle involvement on the part of the spectator. With obvious cyclopean references, Barry turns the tables on the typical art-viewing situation by creating a sculpture that watches the spectator. In *Polythemus,* a massive horizontal cone rides atop a motorized pivoting assembly. The flat end of the cone is spanned by a rear-projection screen. As a viewer enters the room, an electric eye on the piece senses his presence and rotates the cone to look at the intruder. Simultaneously, a projection of one large eye appears on the screen as if to examine the visitor. After a mere five seconds, the eye blinks as the cone turns away. Explaining that the average viewing time for any given work of art in a gallery is five seconds, Barry reverses this relationship by creating an artwork that echoes this same short attention span. *Polythemus* typifies Barry's repetitive use of the cone shape which is based upon the geometric volume formed by projected light.

The confrontational nature of *Polythemus* remains consistent in a subsequent work entitled *Poseidon* (1988). The behemoth machine is forty-four feet long and features a revolving horizontal shaft which runs its entire length. Situated at measured, spiraling intervals along the shaft are a series of six pie-shaped rear-projection screens that increase proportionately in size. Located at the far end is a projector, at the other end a platform for the viewer. When a viewer mounts this platform, the work automatically comes to life. The shaft begins to revolve, bringing the adjacent screens progressively into the line of projection. The film image, a close-up of a groping hand, appears to move through space toward the viewer at an ever increasing size. The sequential approach of the hand becomes wavelike in feeling, and the effect is heightened by the viewer platform simultaneously rocking, upsetting both visually and with motion the viewer's equilibrium.

Clearly, Barry's work demands a certain commitment on the part of the spectator. Upsetting the typically passive viewer-art object relationship, Barry's work invites and depends on physical interaction. The work also upsets the traditional passive relationship between movie viewer and movie. Barry's works are large scale – they confront the viewer in human size and induce an air of domination within the gallery setting.

Recently, Barry moved beyond the gallery setting to further exaggerate his "precinematic movie projector" investigation. During the summer of 1988, the artist received a residency award to create an outdoor sculpture at New York State's famed ARTPARK in Lewiston. Situated along the Niagara River just downstream of the falls, ARTPARK has been a haven for

PHOTO BY STEVE BARRY

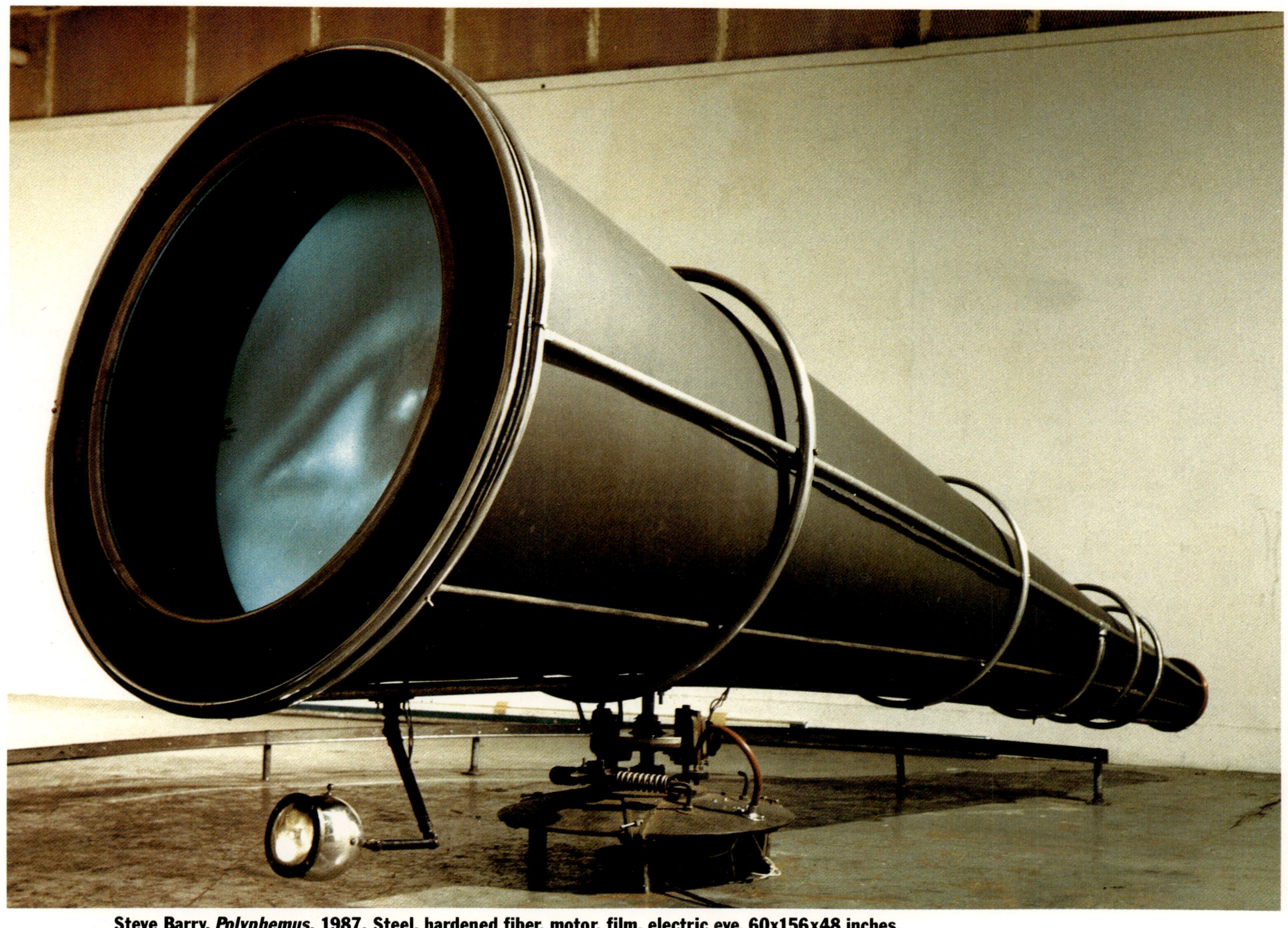

Steve Barry, *Polyphemus,* 1987. Steel, hardened fiber, motor, film, electric eye. 60x156x48 inches. As a viewer enters the room an electric eye senses his presence and rotates to look at the intruder. A large projected eye views the viewer for a few seconds, blinks, and then turns away.

outdoor installation works since its inception in the 1970s. Barry's contribution to ARTPARK was *Aeolus.* The piece's title was derived from a tale in which Odysseus lands on the island of *Aeolus,* the king of winds. The king plays host to Odysseus to hear the story of Troy. As a parting gift, Aeolus bestows upon Odysseus a bag containing the winds and sends up a fair breeze as well to aid the journey homeward.

Barry's *Aeolus* is designed to generate a cinematic image using only natural power sources; the sun provides light for image illumination, and the wind powers mechanical motion for the image movement. The focal point of the work is a towering American farm windmill, whose spinning vanes capture the wind and provide the power for the mechanism. On the ground below lies the Barry trademark cone, measuring a huge eight feet in diameter at its wide end, within which a projected image of a wind-blown human form ("the personification of wind," in the words of the artist) is enlarged. At the small end of the cone, an arrangement of mirrors directs the sunlight through the piece, passing the array of revolving transparencies.

Barry's "mechanical performances" bridge the chronological extremes of Western Man's storytelling tradition. By addressing the ancient oral legacy of Greek mythology, Barry draws upon imagery presumably founded in actual experience and greatly enhanced by the imaginations of untold generations of storytellers to include sirens and one-eyed monsters. At the other end of the storytelling tradition lies the twentieth century's cinematic medium. Charlton Heston has declared film "the dominant art form of the twentieth century." Few will deny the impact of cinema upon the arts. Barry explores it. By requiring the viewer to become involved in the activation of his works and their grand reenactment of mythological epics, Barry is creating a hybrid role for machine-as-storyteller and conveyer of images.

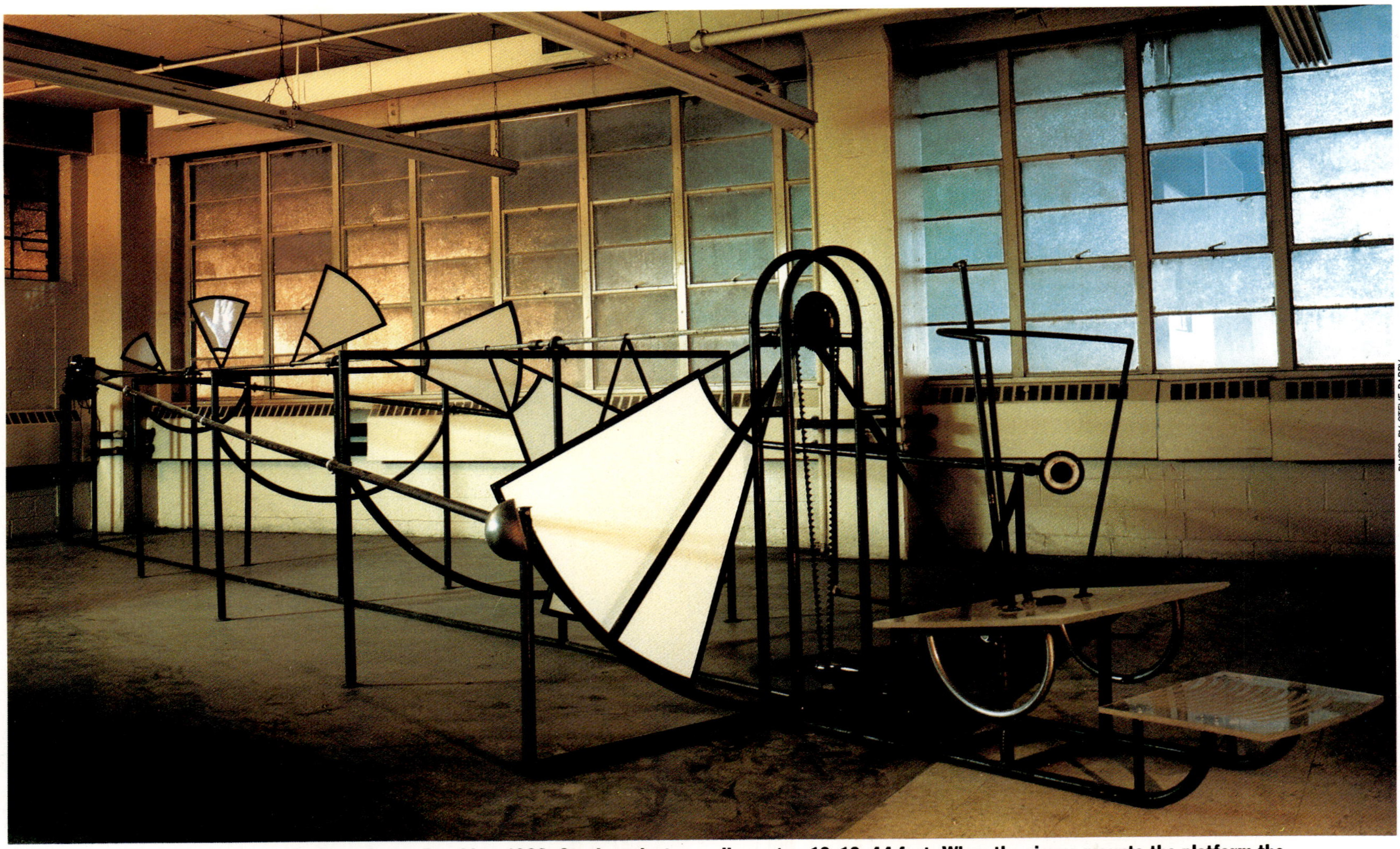

PHOTO BY STEVE BARRY

Steve Barry, ***Poseidon,*** **1988. Steel, projector, audio, motor. 10x10x44 feet. When the viewer mounts the platform the pie-shaped projection screens begin to turn and an image of a groping hand moves toward the viewer.**

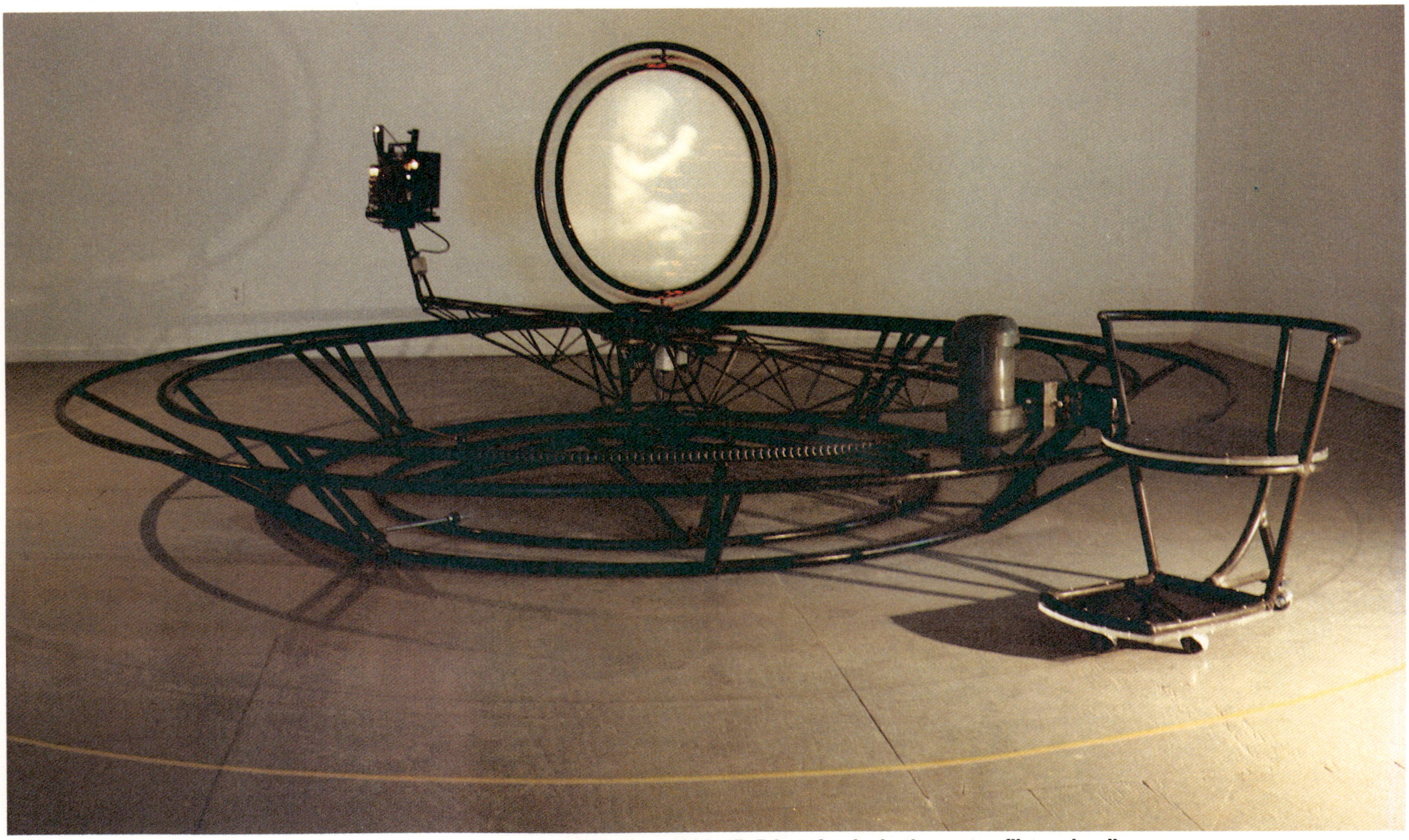

Steve Barry, ***Palladium,*** **1989. 15x5 feet. Steel, plastics, motor, film, and audio.**
Activated by the viewer sitting down on the seat, the machine then rotates the viewer around the perimeter of the piece backwards. In the center stands a projection of a human fetus, which the viewer is forced to view from 360 degrees. The Palladium was a statue constructed by the goddess Athena bearing her own likeness.

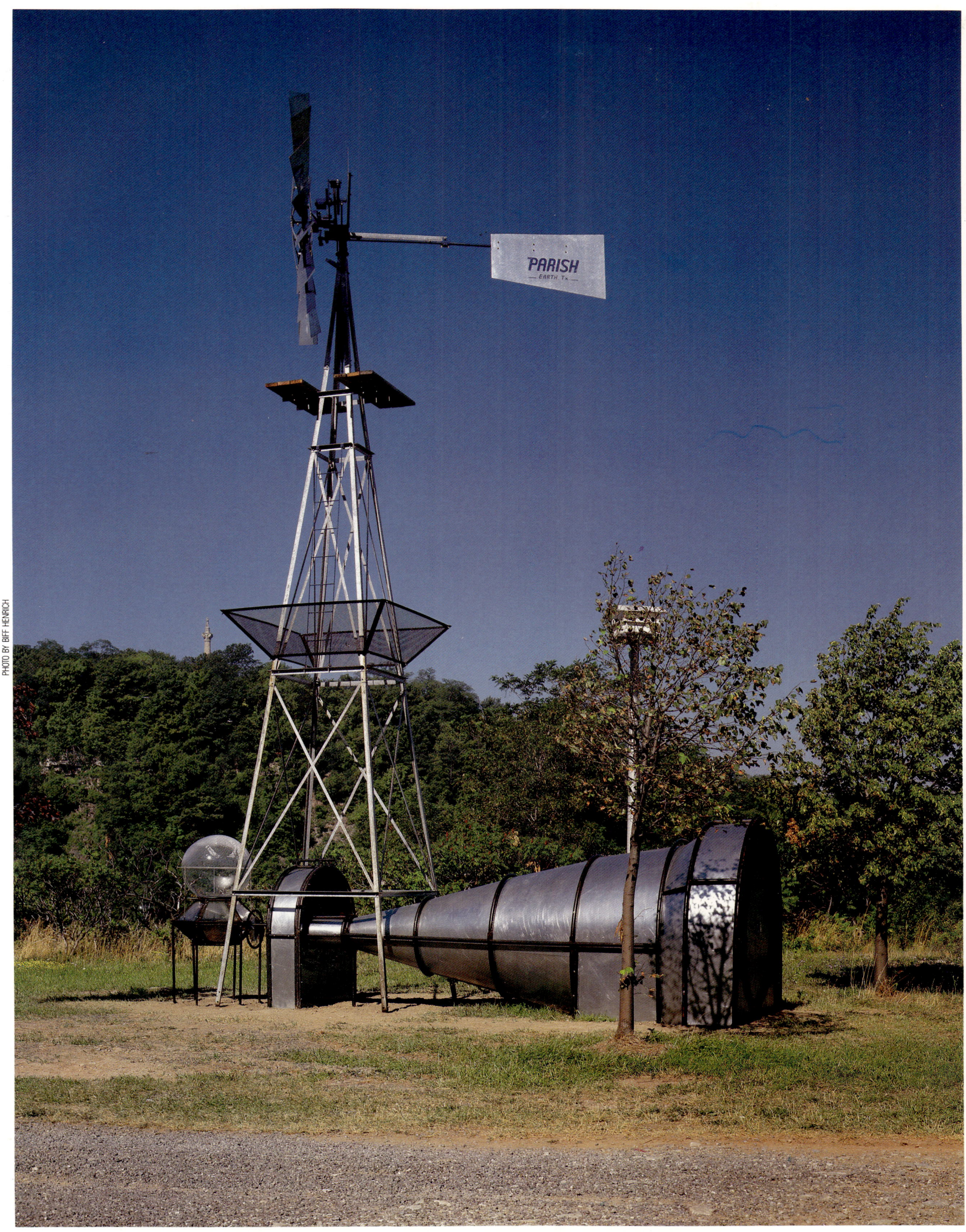

PHOTO BY BIFF HENRICH

Steve Barry, *Aeolus,* 1988. The wind powers the mechanics for projecting an image of a wind-blown human form at the large end of the cone. The sun provides the light source for the projection.

Matthew Gil

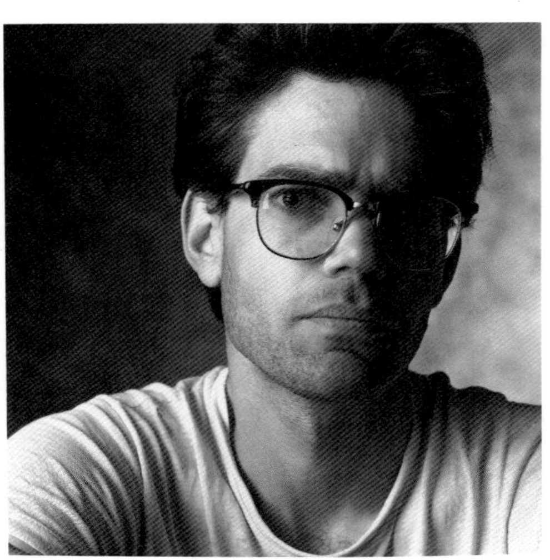

ONE-AND-ONE-HALF HOURS NORTH OF San Francisco is the Napa Valley town of Rumsey. Pioneer Matthew Gil finds refuge here, building his own intaglio press, brewing his own beer, harvesting almonds from his rural property, and fabricating kinetic sculpture. Having lived and worked in San Francisco for years, Gil finally decided to exchange the clutter of city life for the spaciousness of the country. In Rumsey, Gil continues his uninterrupted career as an artist which began in high school, when he would help weld sculptures for a local San Francisco artisan to be sold to tourists at Fisherman's Wharf. Later a student and assistant of noted Bay Area kineticist Fletcher Benton, Gil used Benton's passage through the world of kinetics as a gauge for his own experience, career, and education. Gil credits Benton with helping him become less laborious and more spontaneous in regard to his sculpture.

"Spontaneity is how I get the feeling for the work. I don't even think about the mechanics anymore, it's so secondary to the piece. It's more the whole outlook and external feeling of the piece, or the colors, or the form that is really what you're going to see."

Gil's work is truly as spontaneous as the fabrication of mechanical pieces can be. Surrounding himself with a battalion of metal and motors, Gil is able to attack his work in much the same way as a painter armed with a full palette of paint. Such creative fury may result in the completion of an entire piece within one day – a fervor reminiscent of David Smith's staggering display of production during his residency at Italy's Spoleto Festival in 1962 in which the late sculptor created twenty-six sculptures in just thirty days. Gil's finished work also reflects this frenzied energy. Like the methods of a 1940s Abstract Expressionist, Gil's eye is keyed to the basic formal qualities that direct the viewer through the avenues of color, form, and composition. His imagery recalls the paintings of Miró and the paper cuttings of Matisse. Differing, however, from his predecessors, Gil's forms are captured in geometric composition only to be set free again by motion. Unlike most of the other artists discussed in this book, the narrative in Gil's work is subtly incorporated, giving way to a strong formalist approach.

Kinda Blue is a prime example of Gil's unique style. This larger-than-life-size sculpture features a collection of double-sided squares arranged in vertical rows. Resting atop a pair of spindly legs, the sculpture brings to mind the 1950s modern style of design. The motion of the work is orchestrated by a clever drive system comprised of a series of springs that link the motor to the rows of squares. As the motor slowly spins, the springs first coil themselves up only to soon release, causing the rows of shapes to spin erratically. Since the rows are themselves linked by springs, the

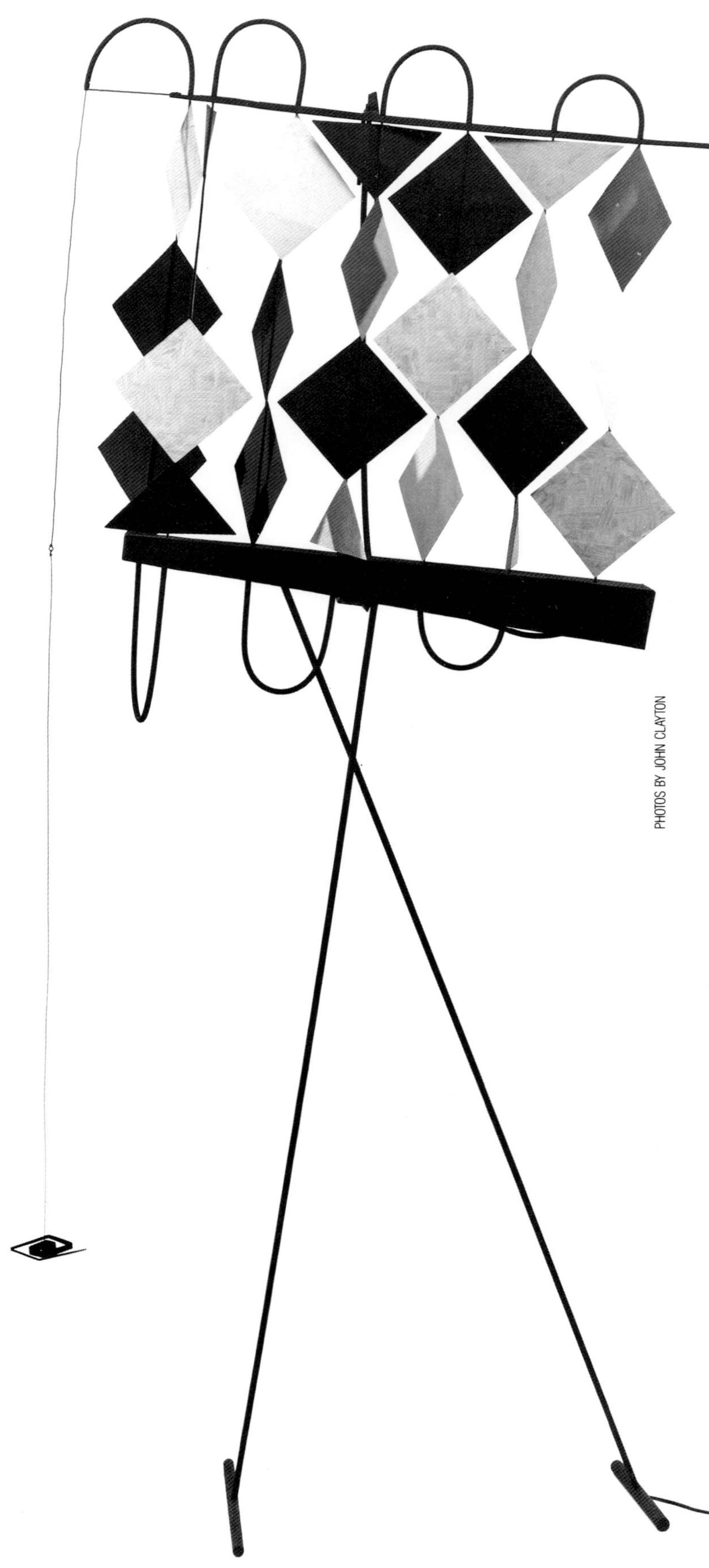

PHOTOS BY JOHN CLAYTON

Matthew Gil, *Kinda Blue,* 1986. Steel, motor, and paint. 84x30x14 inches. The rows of geometric shapes spin randomly as they are released by springs tied to the motor.

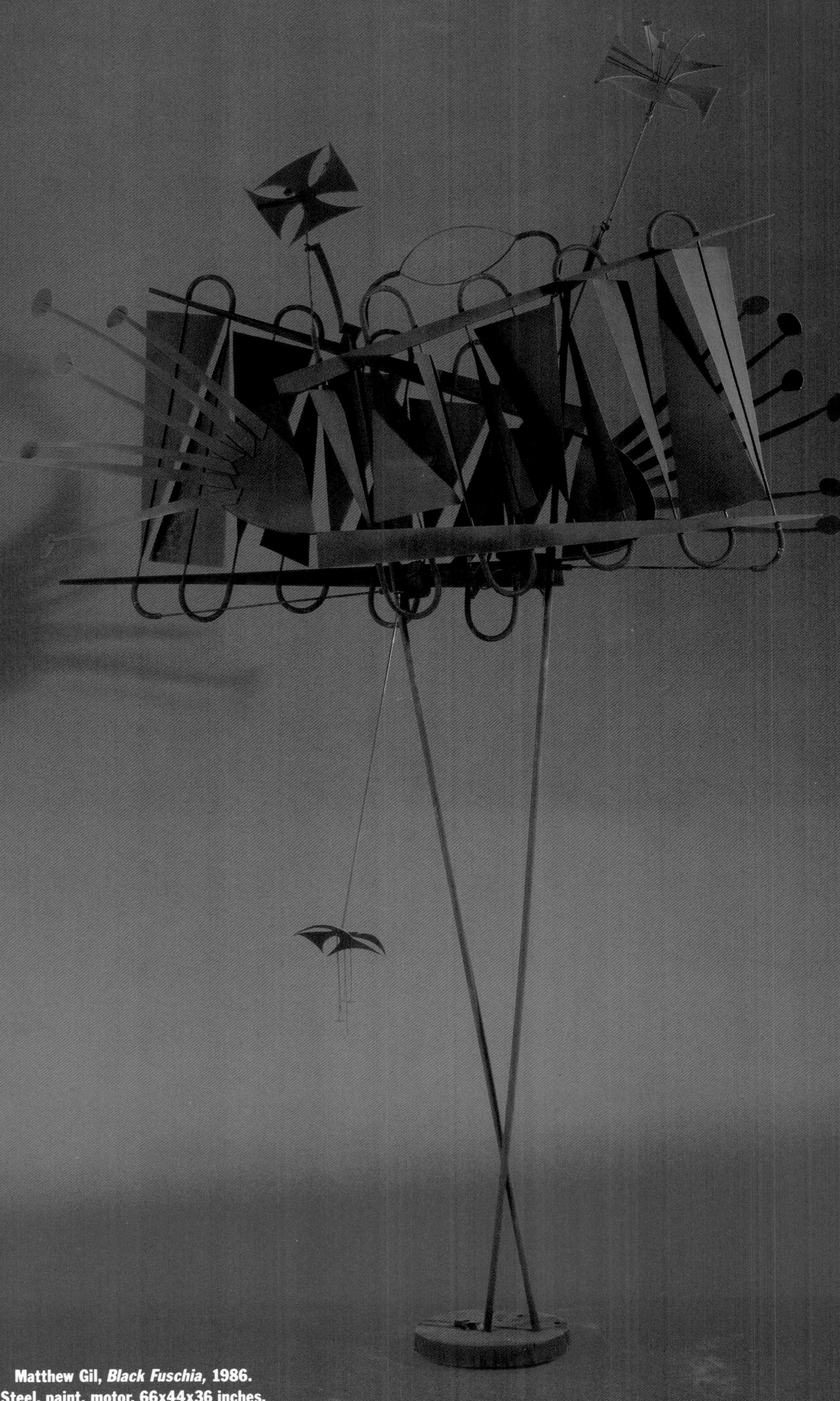

COURTESY IVORY/KIMPTON GALLERY

Matthew Gil, *Black Fuschia,* 1986.
Steel, paint, motor. 66x44x36 inches.

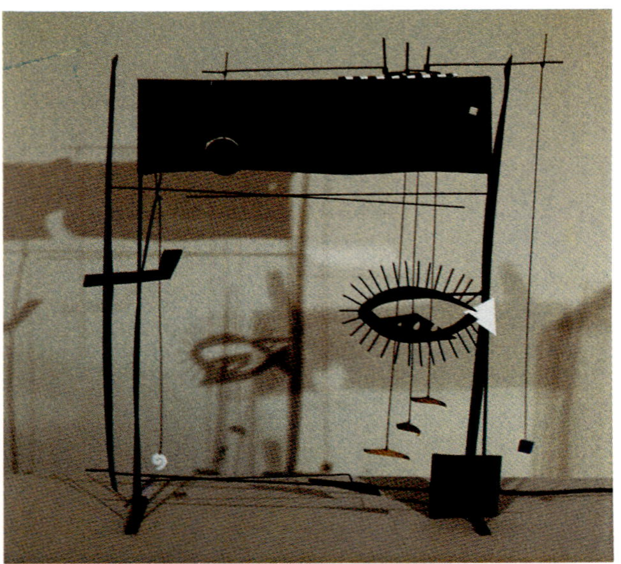

Matthew Gil, *Nova Fish,* 1985. Steel, paint, motor. 24x24x4 inches. The large fish remains static while the rest of the stylized ocean scene moves about as if caught in undersea currents.

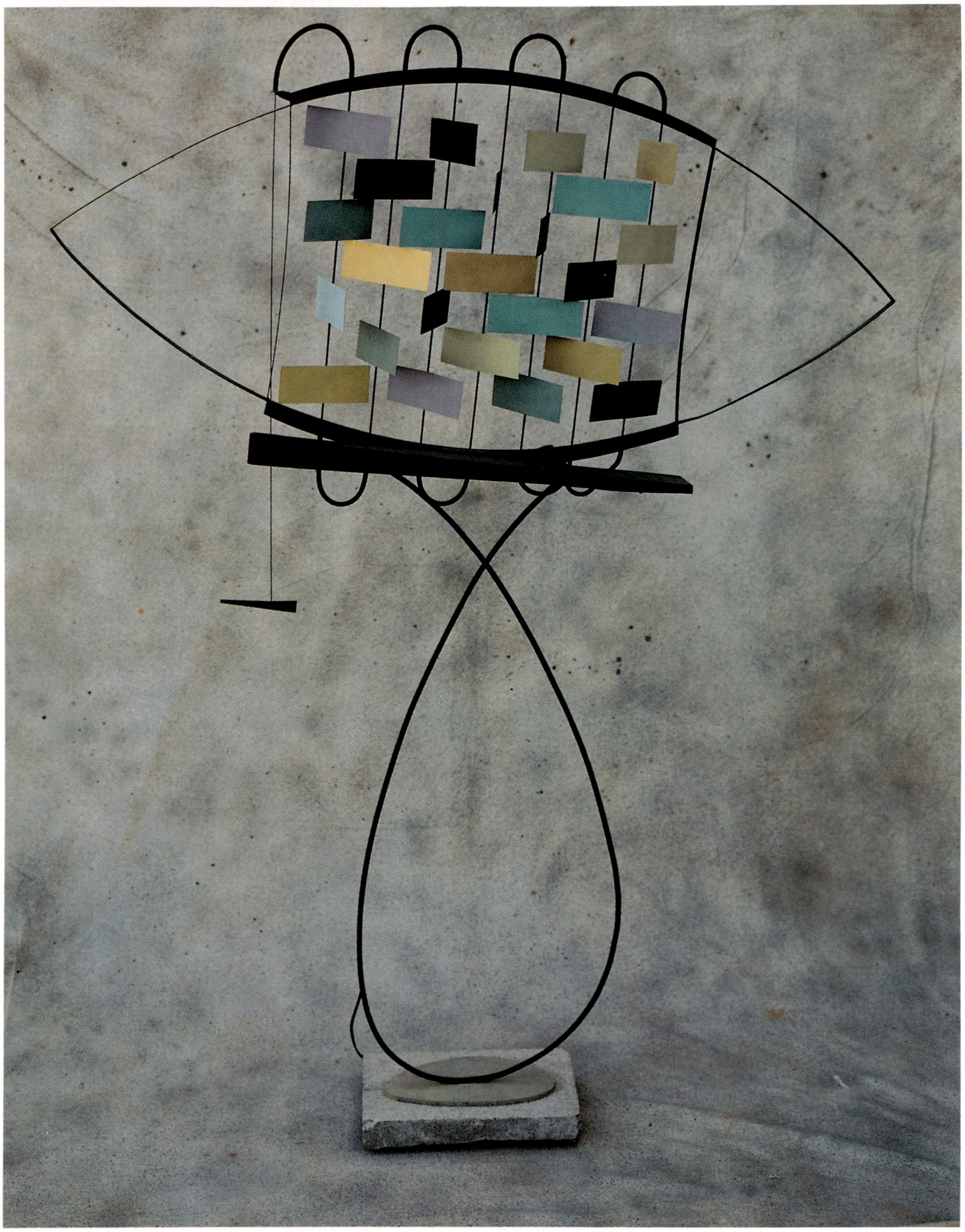

Matthew Gil, *Visica Pisces,* 1986. Steel, paint, motor. 78x54x16 inches. A collection of spring-driven squares is framed by an outline of a fish.

PHOTOS BY JOHN CLAYTON

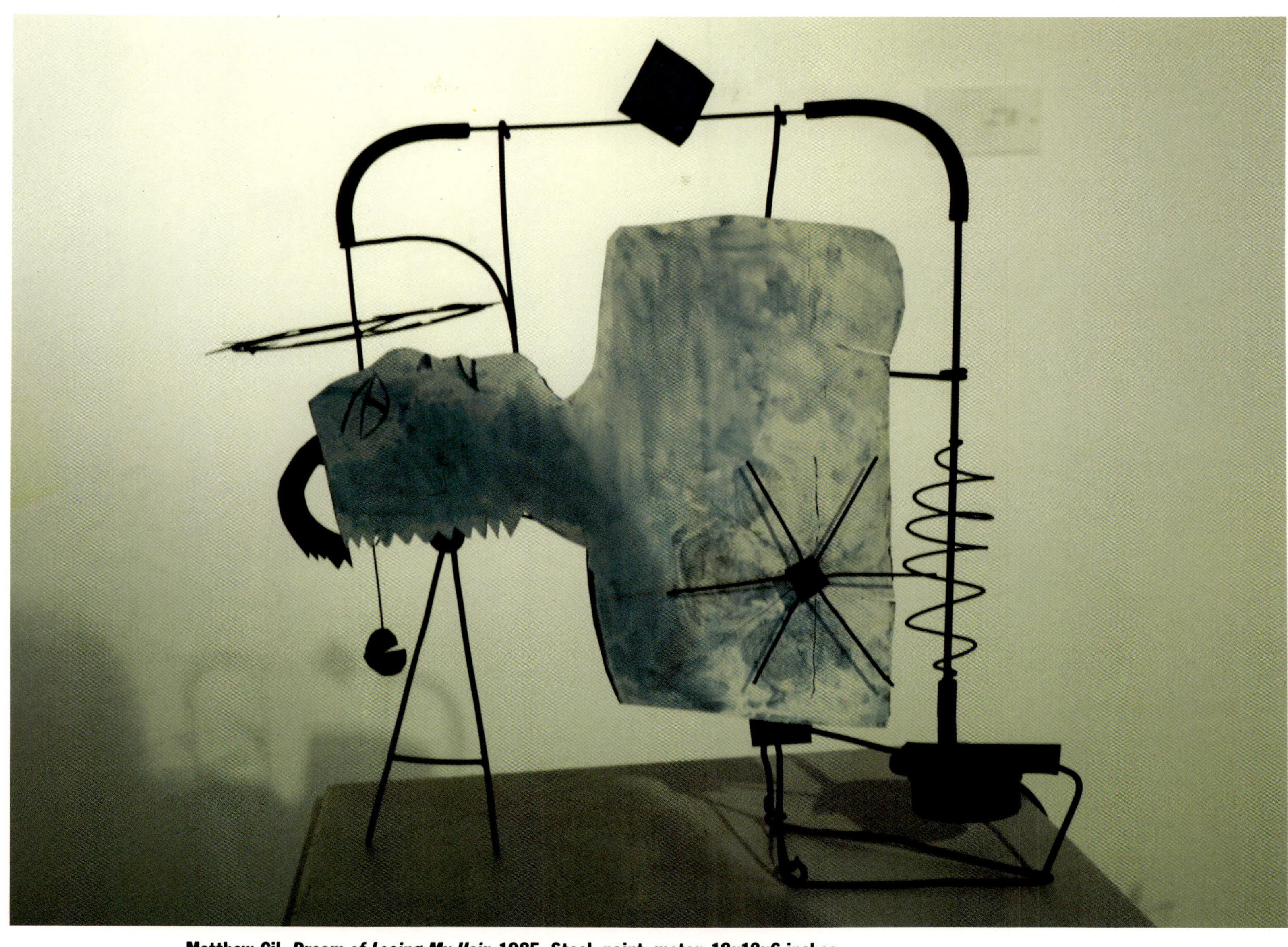

Matthew Gil, *Dream of Losing My Hair,* 1985. Steel, paint, motor. 18x18x6 inches. The disturbed reclining figure is assaulted by spinning pointed spokes.

entire operating sequence of the work is random, unpredictable. In an effort to achieve an organic and natural motion through synthetic means, Gil abandons the staccato rhythm of a work controlled by a programmable timer in favor of a totally sporadic mode of motion. As a result, Gil is successful in creating a machine with antimachine qualities.

"It's not the mechanics, but the movement I'm interested in and I'd get rid of the motors if I could."

In *Visica Pisces,* a similar collection of spring-driven squares is framed by an outline of a fish. In this work, Gil links his totally abstract approach to another direction of interest, the image of the fish. Gil explains that use of the fish is seeded in his childhood. While yearning to own fish as a child, he never did. As a result, these surrogate "aquariums" now represent one dominant motif.

Referred to as "fish frames," these works have a characteristically frontal vantage point. (The fish series has much of the same two-dimensional feel as did David Smith's "steel drawings.") In *Nova Fish,* an arrangement of thin rods and sheet metal cut-out shapes takes on the stylized appearance of a stencil-like oceanic scene. In operation, the focal point of the work, one large lone fish, remains static as the environs surrounding it twist and sway as if caught in some underwater current. While Gil's earlier, more voluminous works dealt with the positive image these more linear works deal with the negative. As the early works featured the interaction of heavy shapes, later works use line to describe these volumes, affording the work a special delicateness. The sole use of black paint on many of these works helps to increase their visual weight.

Aquatic waves translate into brain waves as a third direction of Gil's work explores human psychological complexities. One of Gil's more narrative works, *A Dream of Losing Your Hair,* depicts the reclining head and shoulders of a figure. Painted in the same rough-hewn style as a prehistoric pictograph, the poor soul has an expression of awkward anger. Above its head spins a halo of pointed shards, while a spindly, six-pointed star does the same in the region of the heart. These kinetic elements collectively create an aura of mental unrest imparted onto the ungrateful victim. This sculpture recalls a scene from Fritz Lang's 1931 thriller, *M,* in which the German filmmaker utilizes a collection of manic Duchampian roto-reliefs in a display window to frame the head of a fleeing child murderer, portrayed by Peter Lorre, echoing Lorre's gradual slide into hysteria.

The "figurative landscapes," as Gil refers to his psychological works, are more personal and emotion driven than his other works. Though the style of construction is consistent with his other work, the impact of the imagery evokes a more spiritual frame of mind and presents a greater interpretive challenge to the viewer.

When asked why motion is chosen to depict these and other personal situations, Gil replies, "Things that move have always attracted me more... because everything I see actually moves, and thus my eye defines things in these terms. Ever since I was a kid I have noticed the inherent state of change."

Andrew Ginzel/Kristin Jones

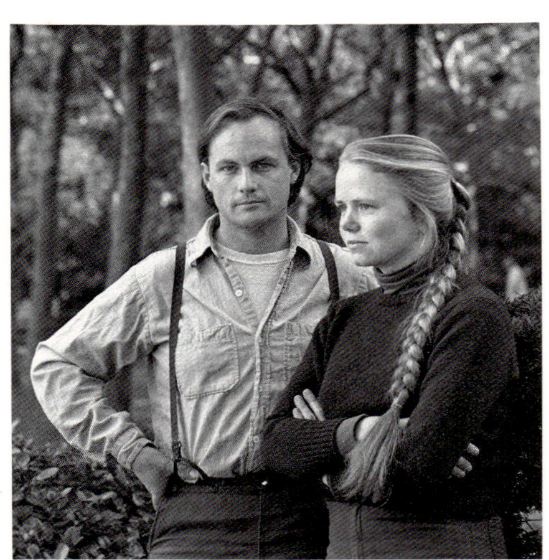

THE ELABORATE INSTALLATION DIoramas of New York artists Andrew Ginzel and Kristin Jones address elemental visual investigations of the Cosmos – a metaphorical engagement of humanity's epic search into the mysteries of outer space, inner space, the mind, and the forces of the micro-macro universe both seen and unseen. Ginzel and Jones draw upon a rich visual tradition as old as the unnamed ancient artists who connected the brighter magnitude "star dots" to created the Greek constellations, and as new as the extraordinary moon and planet images Voyager II has radioed to Earth along is epic interplanetary journey – arguably the most monumental images provided by science in our lifetimes.

Penumbra, installed in 1985 at the Clocktower space in New York City, is representative of Ginzel and Jones's cosmic tableau installations. A postcard-size aperture revealed the scenario to the viewer. The actual installation was constructed within a 9-by-12-by-30-foot room. In the foreground was the domed top of an enormous blue globe with dots of light flickering on its surface. Behind it, light beams radiated through a fine vapor, a jet of water shot an arc from left to right, and particles of water fragmented in fiery jewels. Steam rose and dotted blue rings of flame burned in the distance. A red ribbon spit a stream of fire in the background. Minute points of violet light shone through the darkness. In sum, the small aperture was the eyepiece of the telescope, and the view was one of celestial images in constant movement, constant change.

Spheric Storm, installed at New York City's Art Galaxy in 1985, transformed a gallery into a streetfront theatre. Passing pedestrians could look into the gallery through an 18-by-25-inch window. Inside, a four-minute cycle presentation commenced with complete darkness. The action developed gradually from the black void into a dramatic crescendo of a fully animated intergalactic storm. Light beams played imagery of swirling galaxies. Arc and diode lights flashed as abstractly defined geologic forms rose and eclipsed. The entire diorama ebbed back to black void, its cycle completed only to start anew. In *Spheric Storm,* the cycle is the dominant metaphor – the cycle of star life, human life, all change in the universe which itself may cycle from one Big Bang and expansion to contraction and collapse, only to be reborn with another Big Bang.

With *Pangaea* (1986), a special project for *ARTFORUM* magazine, Ginzel and Jones created astounding visual relationships. Flames, light rays articulated

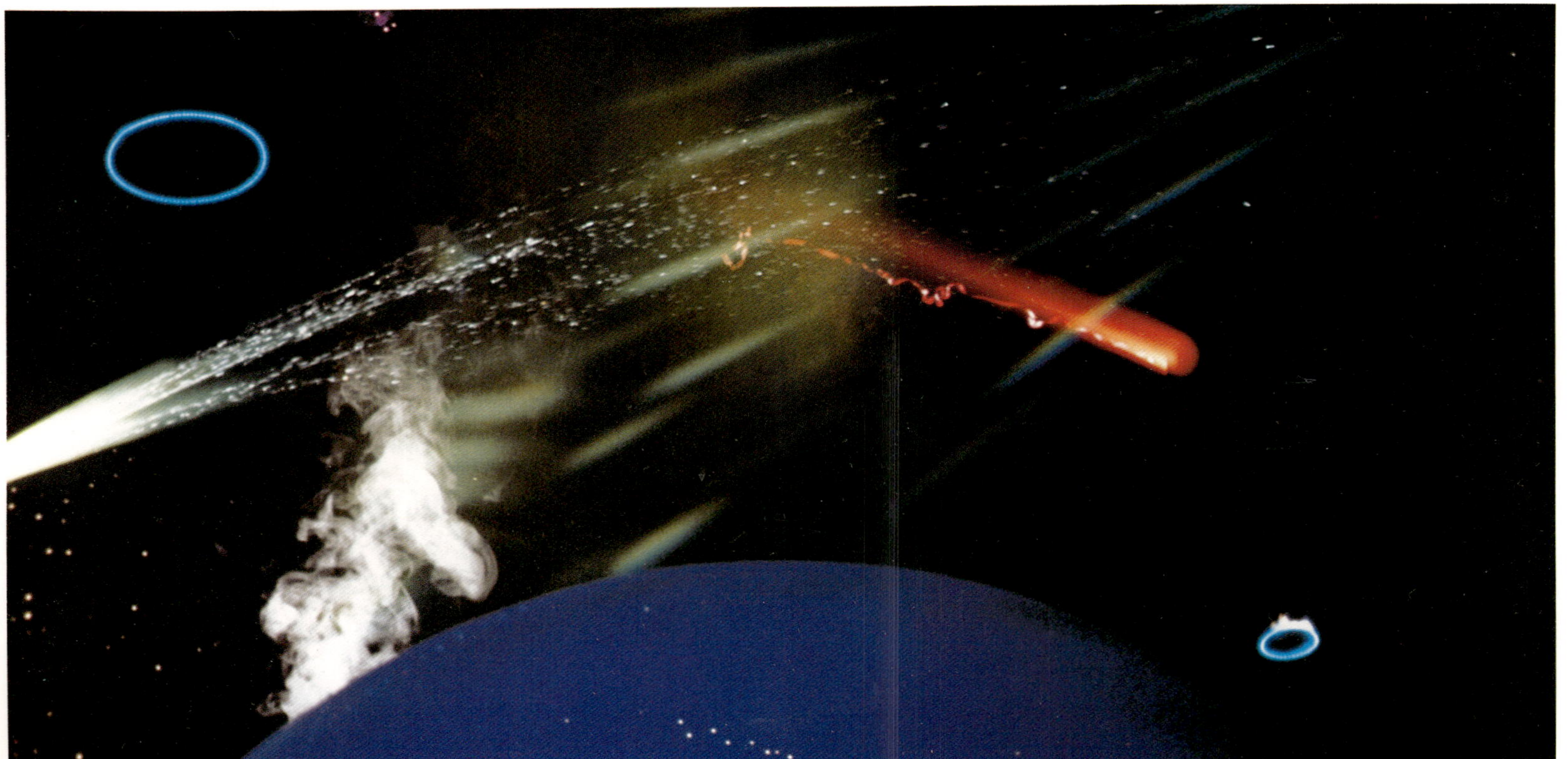

PHOTO BY T. CHARLES ERICKSON

Andrew Ginzel and Kristin Jones, *Penumbra,* 1985. Water, steam, ribbon, steel, blower, incandescent lights, motors, pump, rheostats, propane. 9x12x30 feet. A postcard-sized aperture reveals the scenario inside the room. In the foreground is an enormous blue dome with flickering light on its surface. Behind light beams radiate through a fine vapor of water. Steam rises and dotted blue rings of flame burn in the background. A red ribbon spits a stream of fire in the background.

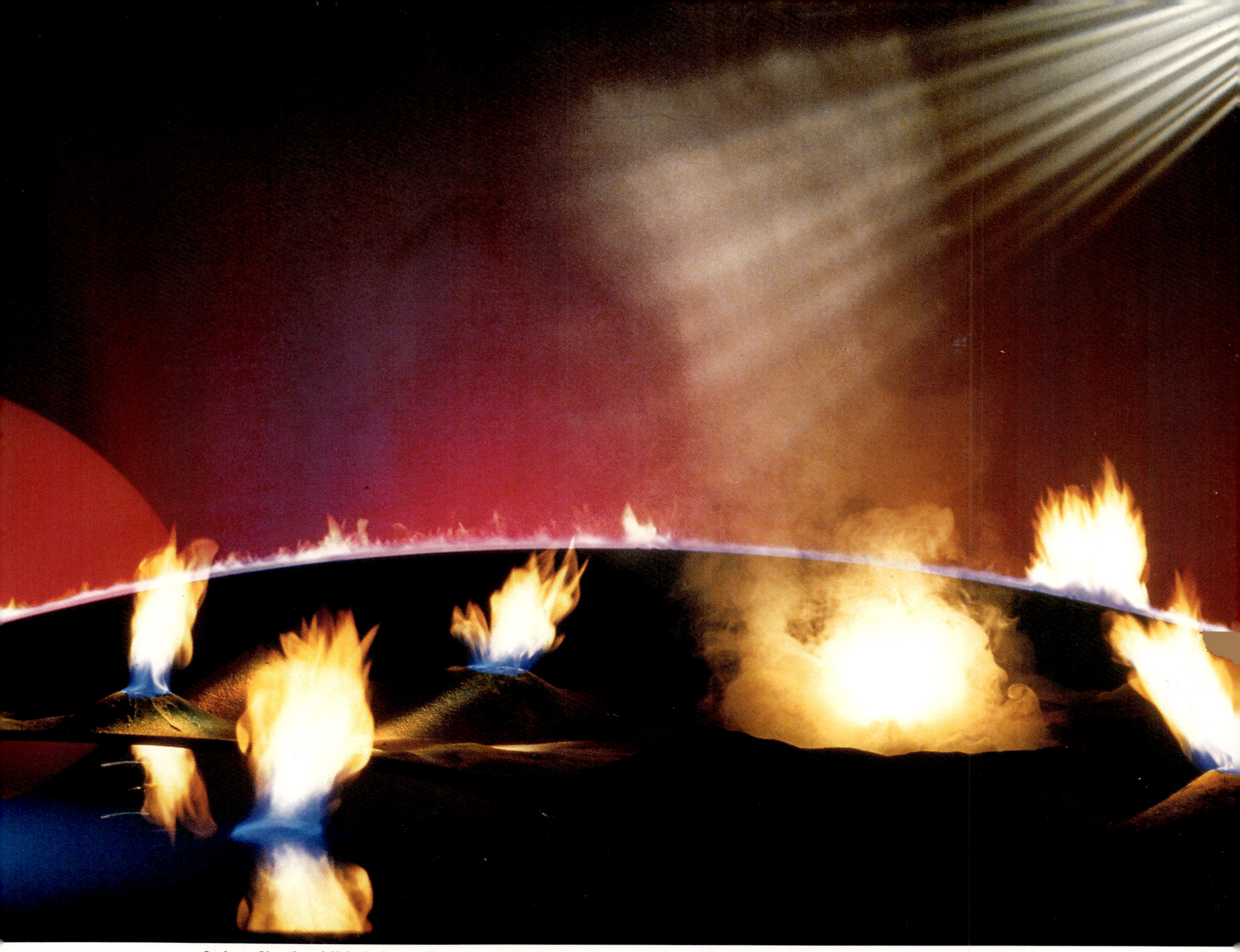

Andrew Ginzel and Kristin Jones, *Pangaea,* 1986. Flames, vapor, sand, water, muslin, balloon, pigment, lights. 9x12x15 feet.

PHOTO BY T. CHARLES ERICKSON

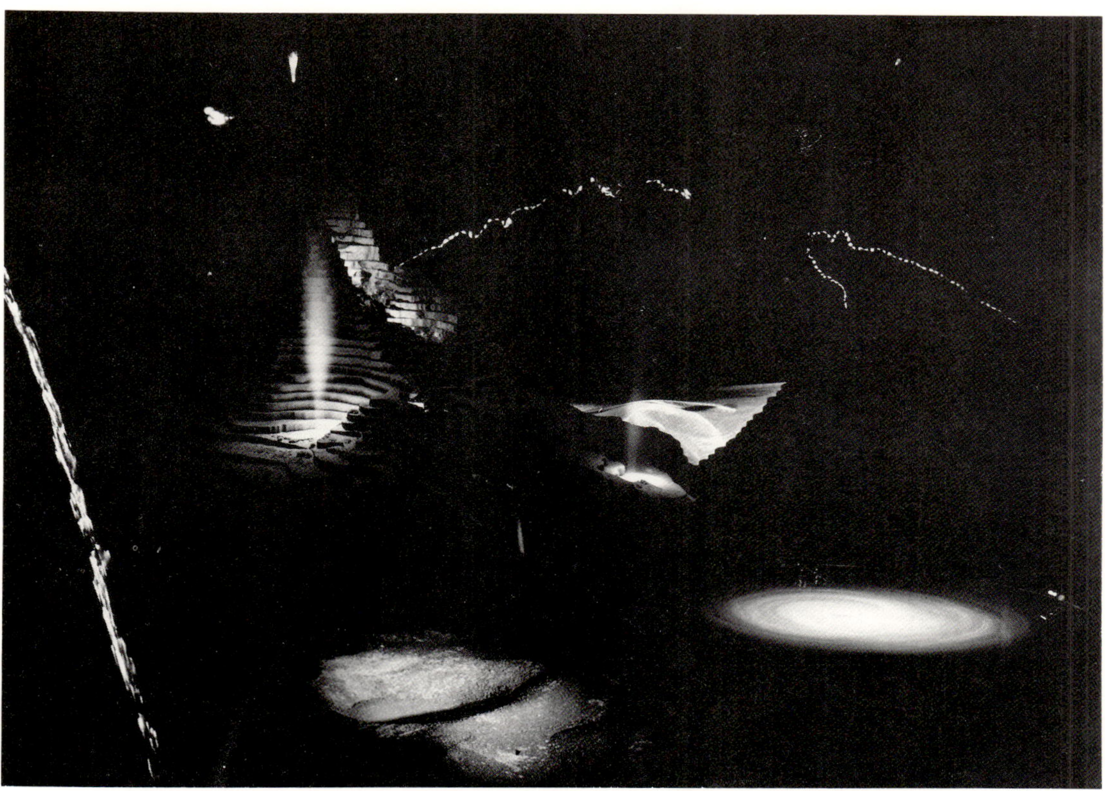

Andrew Ginzel and Kristin Jones, *Spheric Storm,* 1985. Water, sand, pigment, steam, rubber, steel, silk, pumps, motors, timers, blowers, plastics and incandescent, diode, and arc lights. 10x16x31 feet. An 18x25-inch aperture from the street allows viewers to experience a four-minute cycle inside the gallery. The action develops gradually from black void to the dramatic crescendo of a fully animated storm and then back to black again.

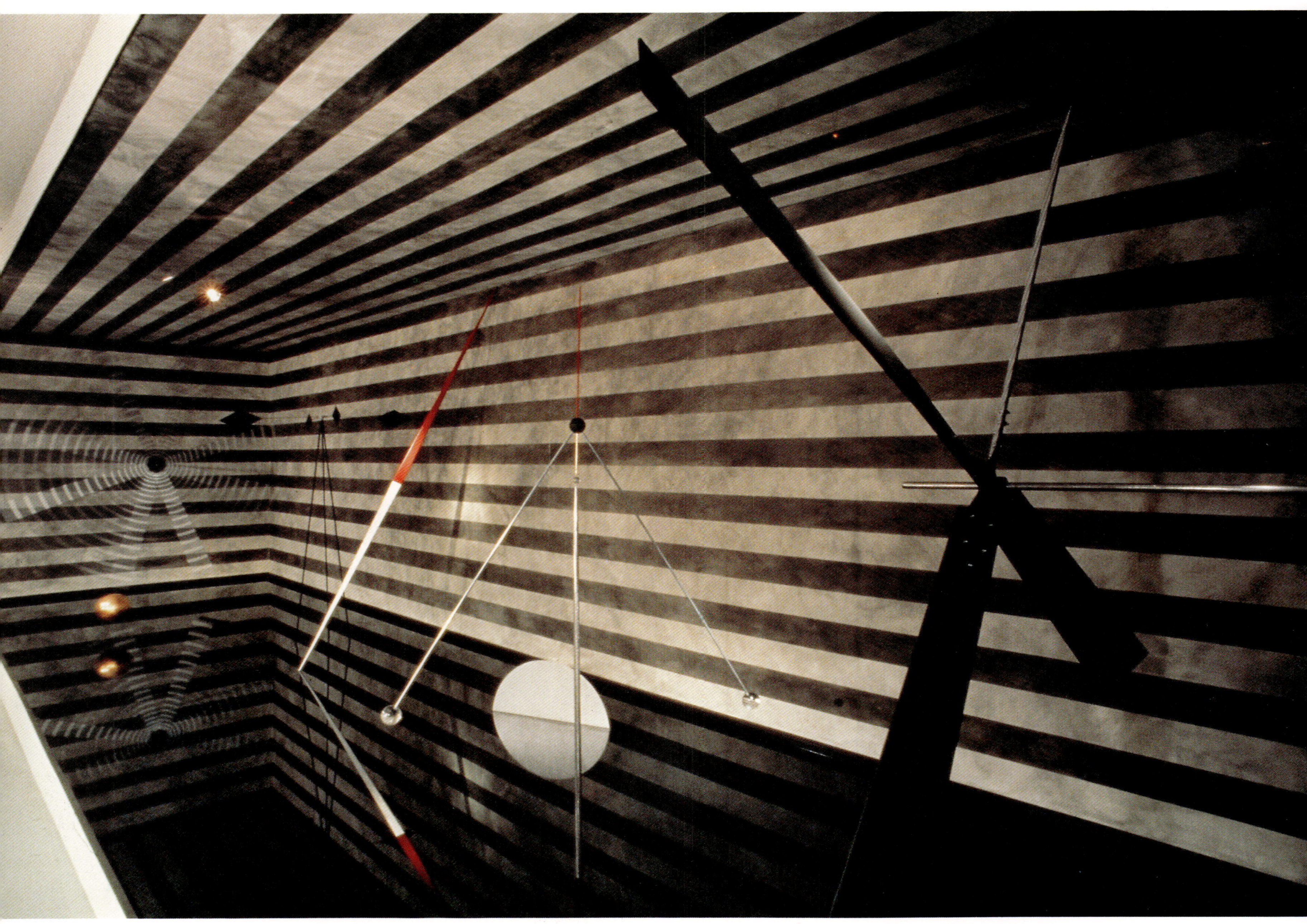

Andrew Ginzel and Kristin Jones, *Vis-a-Vis,* 1987. Wind, water, pigment, pump, motors, timers, wood, aluminum, steel, halogen quartz light, acrylic, bronze, copper, and gold. 8x30x8 feet.

through vapor, and other moving elements conspired to create a miniworld of cosmic conflict.

In their Art Galaxy *Vis-a-Vis* (1987) installation, Ginzel and Jones created a water-air-light ballet of softer emotion. A thirty-foot-long room was defined with elemental gray-and-white stripes. The floor of the room was an inky black reflecting pool into which the roof leaked a constant rain of water drops. Two large propellers varied speeds at either end of the environment. Between them, a menagerie of elemental forms gracefully pursued motion including a six-foot long needle, a copper leaf beach ball, and an abstract weather vane assembly that moved at the caprice of the opposing wind machines. According to Ginzel and Jones, *Vis-a-Vis* is a metaphor for weather – both meteorological and emotional.

Ginzel and Jones's work is metaphoric, poetic, formal – it invites many rich interpretations. There is an overwhelming undercurrent of elemental and historical integrity to their investigations. The Greek's five elements of the universe (Earth, Wind, Air, Fire, and Water) are represented – as is modern science's definition of three states of matter (solid, liquid, and gas). Although their dioramas are clearly three dimensional, they also respect a more formal and traditional painterly two-dimensional format with respect to total composition and a preoccupation with the staid aspects of sphere, line, and plane. Within that format Ginzel and Jones utilize movement to define volume, drawing upon the Greek definition of space as process. It starts with point, as point moves through space it creates line, as line moves through space it creates plane, and as plane moves through space it creates volume.

As with the *Penumbra* and *Spheric Storm* installations, Ginzel and Jones often force the viewer to ac-

PHOTOS BY T. CHARLES ERICKSON

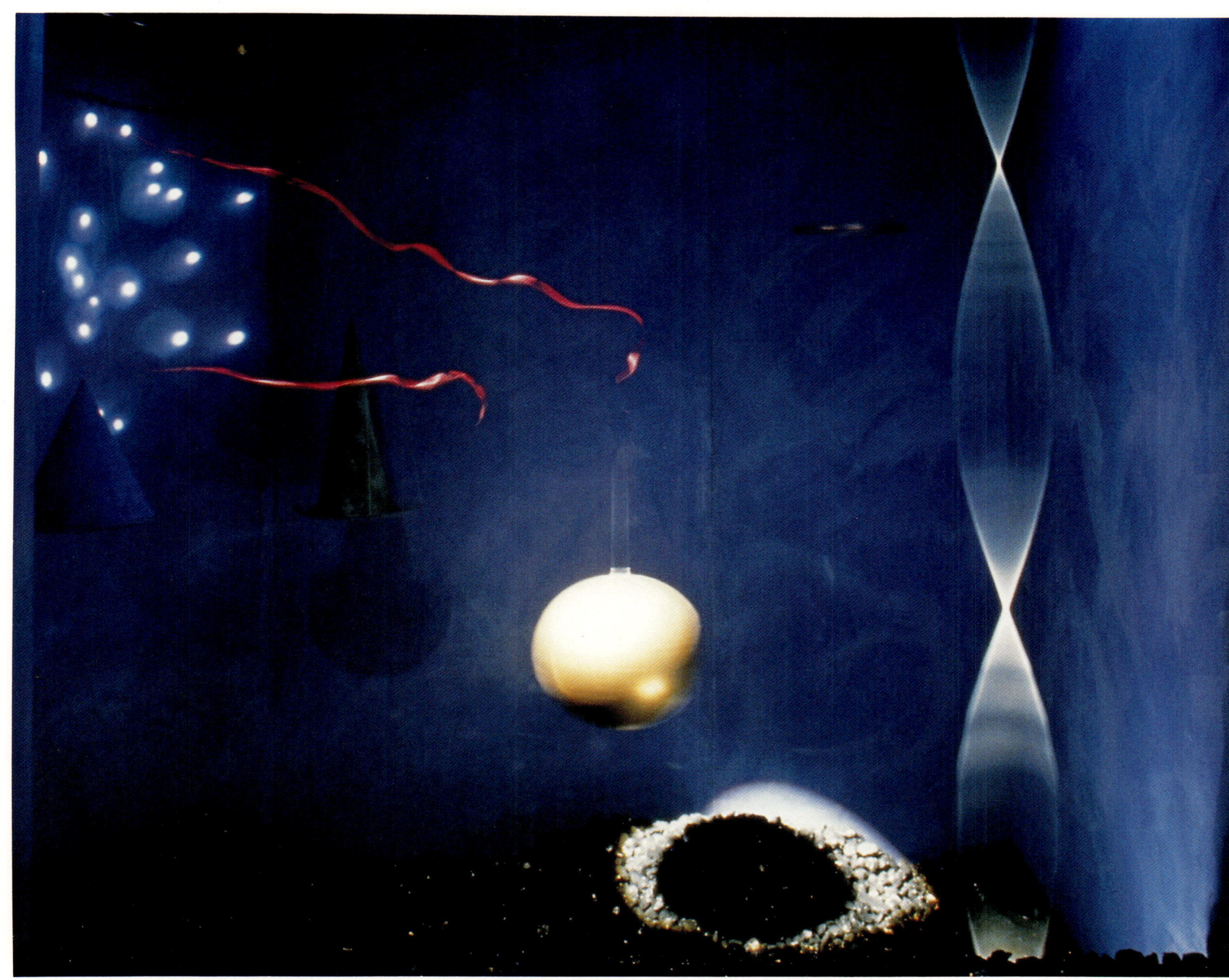

Andrew Ginzel and Kristin Jones, *Clepsydra,* 1986. Water, coal, brass, nylon, pigment, motors, ribbon, electronics, copper, and gold. 9x8x6 feet.

cess their cosmos diorama through a small window. By carefully editing viewer access, the artists distort reference to scale. The actual size of the diorama is a mystery to the viewer – just as the stargazer has no immediate reference to the distance (equals age) of the myriad of individual stars of the Milky Way. In absence of scale, might the viewer be looking into inner space? By creating nonscaled relationships, Ginzel and Jones delve the intrigue that matter orbits – whether it is microelectron matter about the nucleus of the atom (atomic force), or the orbit of moons about planets, planets around suns, and galaxies about one another (gravity force).

Motion is integral to the installations of Ginzel and Jones. The artists' work is distinguished by its elaborate efforts to disguise all reference to machine, opting instead to present motion in the abstract as if originated upon its own (just as it does in the universe, in the atom).

There is a fundamental historical precedent for Ginzel and Jones's use of machine motion to discuss the Cosmos. Since Man's earliest capture of force through machine, two primary assignments of machine have been to record time and the movement of the universe. The Greeks devised kinetic "hydro clocks," the ancients passed sand through the hourglass, and early in the industrial revolution there quickly arose an incredibly complex clock technology. Probably the most intricate machines of the Middle Ages were developed by royal astronomers who sought to predict the movement of the sun, moon, and planets by mechanically recreating their epicycles in the Ptolemaic system with Earth at the center of the Cosmos. Such incredibly precise machines still function today in planetariums, of course with the correction of Earth's proper location.

Everett Greenbalm

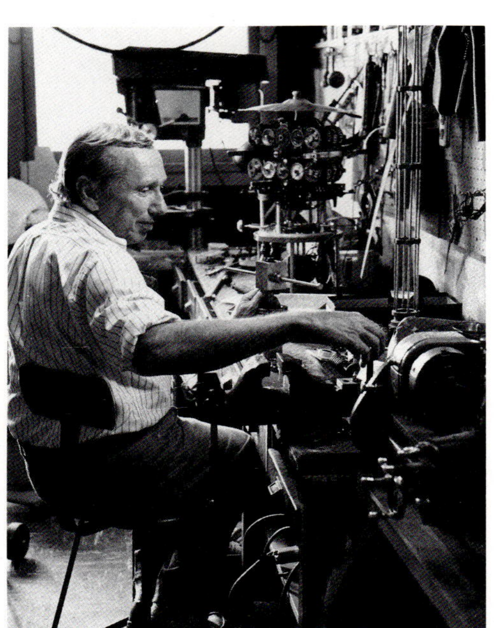

SUCCESS AND ROBUST CREATIVITY are two continuous threads of Everett Greenbalm's forty-year parallel careers as both kinetic artist and Hollywood writer. A lifetime aviator (he first flew in 1934), a student at both MIT and the Sorbonne, Greenbalm's writing credits are legendary: the cult "Mr. Peepers" of the fifties; the "Andy Griffith" TV mainstay of the sixties; scores of "M.A.S.H." episodes in the seventies; and a handful of feature-length movies. Less commercial in nature but equally upbeat in character is the body of kinetic mechanical sculptures Greenbalm has created over the last three decades.

Motion, in all matter of mechanized format, is a constant of virtually all Greenbalm sculpture. Among the most visually striking of Greenbalm's sculptures is *Buckshot Powered Railroad Crossing Alarm* (1973), a Rube Goldbergesque contraption that swings red-and-white checkered arms back and forth and rings bells with the simple power of falling buckshot. When the buckshot supply is exhausted, the viewer must refill the top stainless steel reservoir from the collection canister at the base.

Railroad Crossing is clean in composition, a masterpiece of workmanship, and a precisely coherent assemblage of widely divergent found objects. The work is at one with the technological era that built millions of red-and-white bellringing railroad crossing gates. *Railroad Crossing* is also rich in Greenbalm's love of "machine craftsmanship" – sentimental recall of a heavy industry America where mighty steam-powered locomotives crossed highways at level, rather than with bridges and underpasses.

Greenbalm's affection for an earlier mechanical era is that of wide-eyed wonderment – a young boy who sees his first calliope or plays his first pinball game. This playful, participatory nature surfaces throughout Greenbalm's work. His pieces are each viewer activated. In *EGO Machine* (1988), a viewer-powered hand crank turns two speed governor counterweights, the upward force of which trips a mercury switch which then lights the neon letters "EGO." The work is a moving three-dimensional metaphor that reminds the viewer that personal accomplishment "lights the ego." *EGO Machine* not only utilizes the efforts of the viewer, but also rewards physical strokes with ego strokes.

Tic Toc (1973) is a wonderfully large-scale abstract clock mechanism. The viewer turns the big crank wheel, compacting a huge spring, which then discharges its energy through a clanking rhythmic mechanism. There is no clock per se – Greenbalm is divorcing the time function from the clock mechanism in pure celebration of the mechanism's synchronized movement as an end in and of itself.

The Great American Flag Waving Machine (1970) marches on political turf. Decades ago Greenbalm scavenged a World War I cannon-loading mechanism – it looks something like a tank track. Combining it with a nineteenth-century hand-powered rug stitcher, Greenbalm created a grinding "patriot's" machine that waves a miniature American flag, while bouncing red, white, and blue wooden balls. The work captures an "old-fashioned feeling of patriotism" – a kind of Fourth of July celebration of militarism with

PHOTO BY GEORGE FENNEMAN

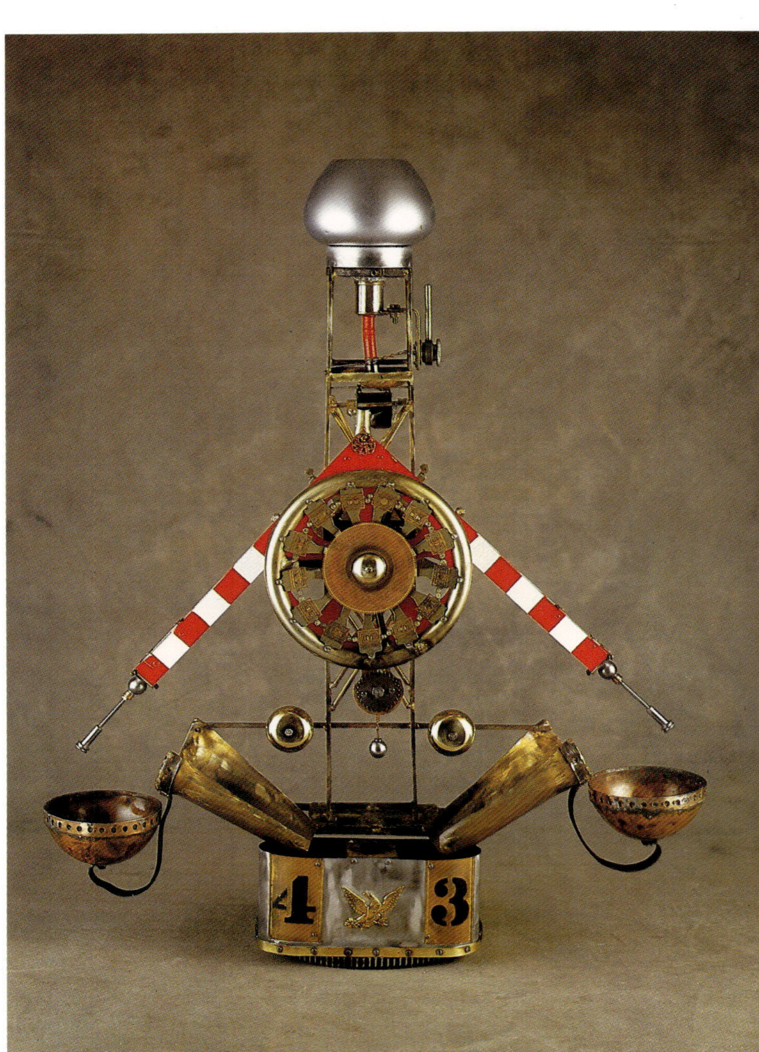

Everett Greenbalm, *Buckshot Powered Railroad Crossing Alarm,* 1973. Aluminum, brass, and steel. 10x16x40 inches. The red and white arms swing and the bells ring, all powered by falling buckshot.

PHOTO BY JEFF ATHERTON

machine parts built to win the "war that would end all wars."

When asked about his involvement with movement, Greenbalm replies: "It's alive." As a writer, he assembles his collective experience into written word not to freeze it as book, but as a means to create living three-dimensional drama on TV and in cinema. As a sculptor, Greenbalm assembles his collective experience, and collected found objects, to create living, moving three-dimensional sculpture.

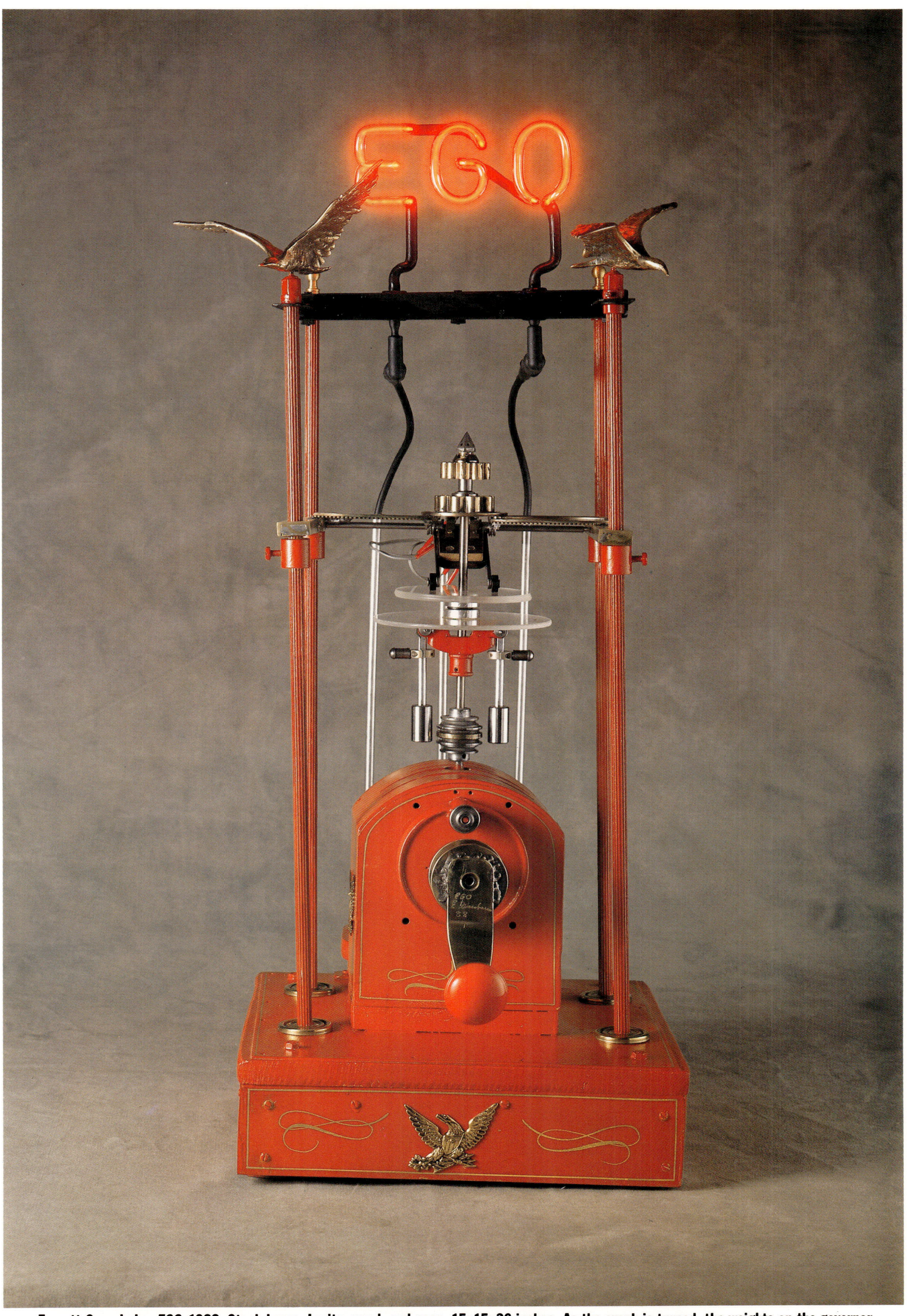

PHOTO BY JEFF ATHERTON

Everett Greenbalm, *EGO,* 1988. Steel, brass, Lucite, wood, and neon. 15x15x36 inches. As the crank is turned, the weights on the governor rise causing mercury switches to close. The word "EGO" lights up as electronic music is heard playing "For He's a Jolly Good Fellow."

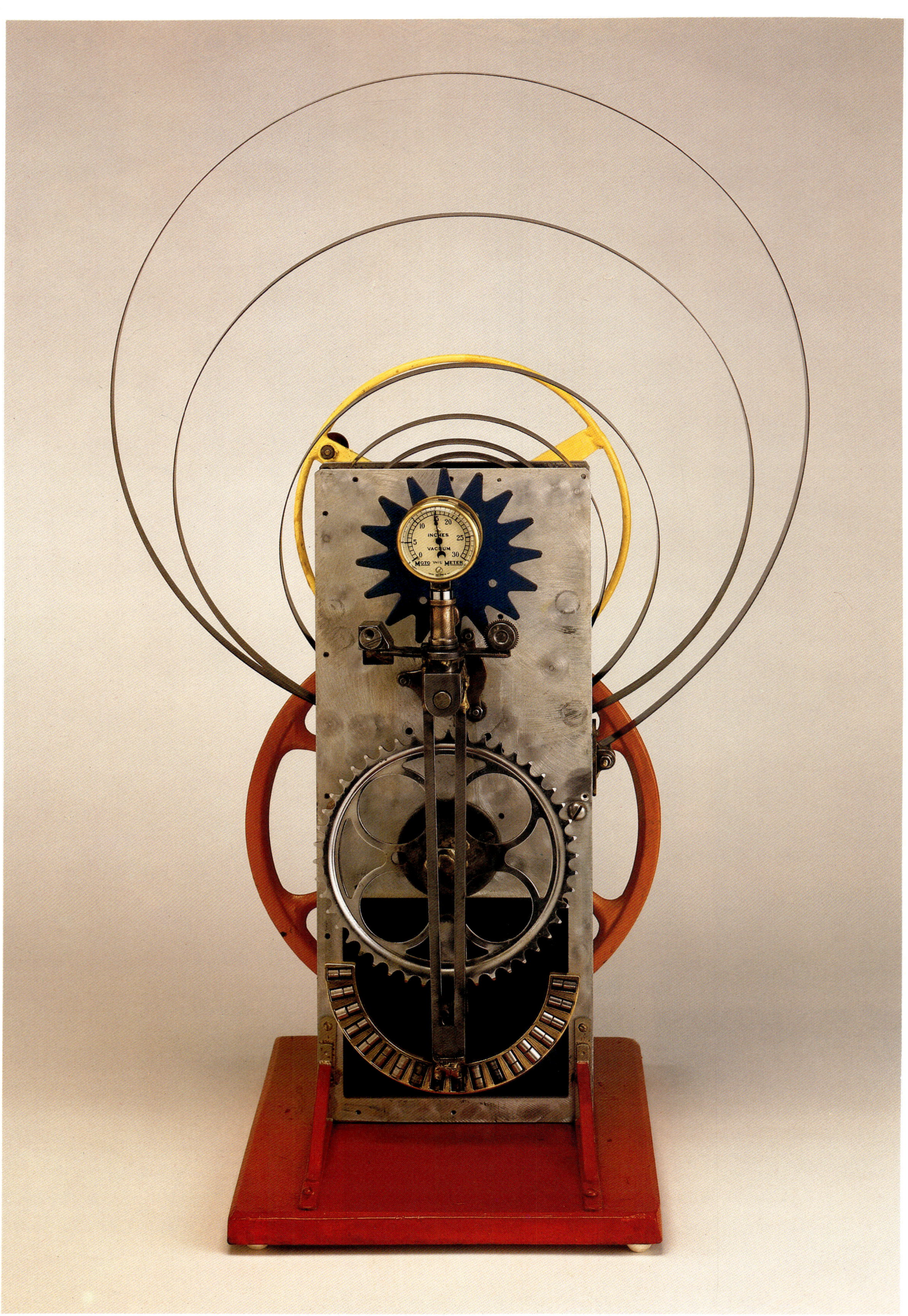

Everett Greenbalm, *Tic Toc,* 1973. Brass, wood, cast iron, and spring steel. 12x16x30 inches. The spring is wound by turning the yellow crank wheel. On release, the large escapement rocks boisterously.

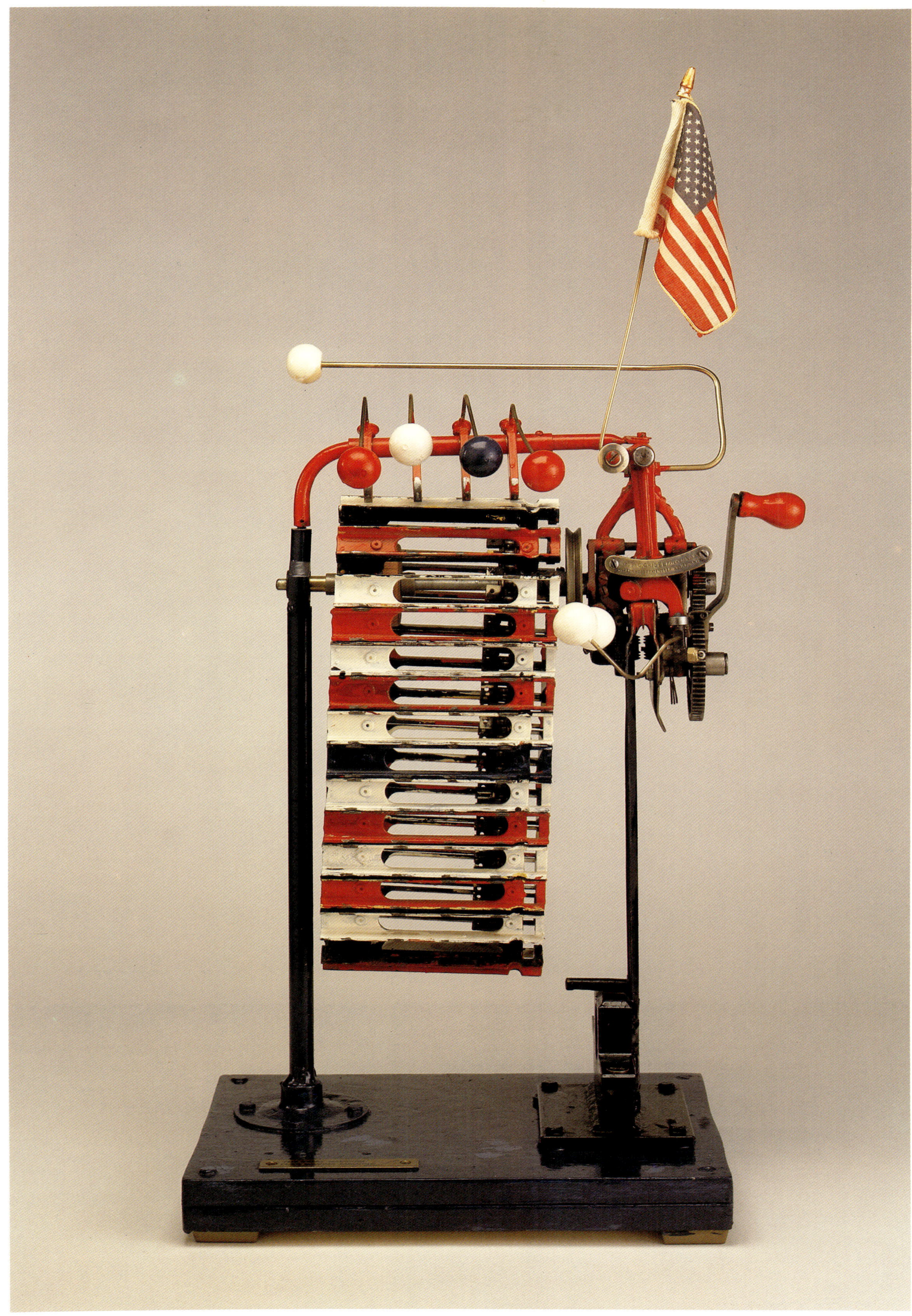

PHOTOS BY JEFF ATHERTON

Everett Greenbalm, *The Great American Flag Waving Machine,* 1970. Cast iron, wood, and brass. 11x16x35 inches. When the crank is turned the red, white, and blue balls move in various patterns. Above it all, Old Glory waves.

Dave Quick

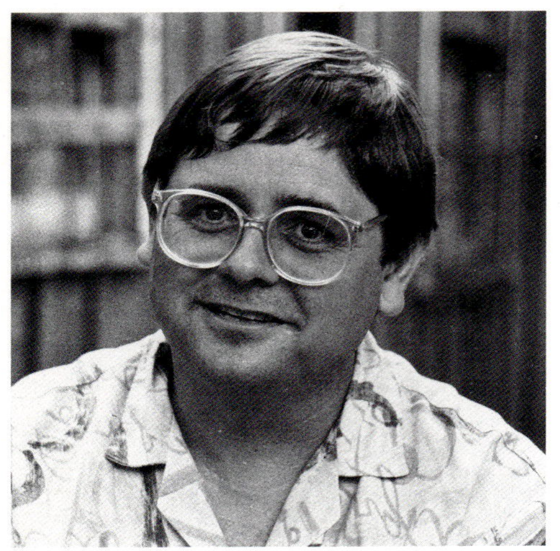

CURRENT EVENTS, ASSEMBLAGE OF found objects, and biting social satire collide in the kinetic sculptures of Dave Quick. Working in a highly narrative, visually entertaining format, Quick creates three-dimensional political and social "sculptural diatribes" whose superficial appeal grates against the gravity of heady topics, including nuclear annihilation, the holocaust, and dehumanization by machine, pornography, and mass culture.

Quick's spoof on the military-industrial complex, *Little Nuke* (1979), is a landmark work within the artist's portfolio. A pathetic rubber chicken has been halved to expose the complex inner workings of an intercontinental bomber. The entire assembly is suspended in a miniature high-tech laboratory complete with three white-smocked lab technicians who scale the setting. On the back wall are six photos of rubber chicken bombers in actual flight. When the viewer pushes "the button," the entire work comes alive. Light shifts from bright fluorescent white to "night vision" red, dials spin, LEDs count furiously, the chicken's rear legs swim back and forth, and from within the bird lowers the atomic bomb plastic egg. As the egg fully descends, an alarm bell rings, "NUCLEAR FISSION – EVACUATE" warns, and a photo flash inside the egg fires. The viewer just died in a nuclear accident of the absurd.

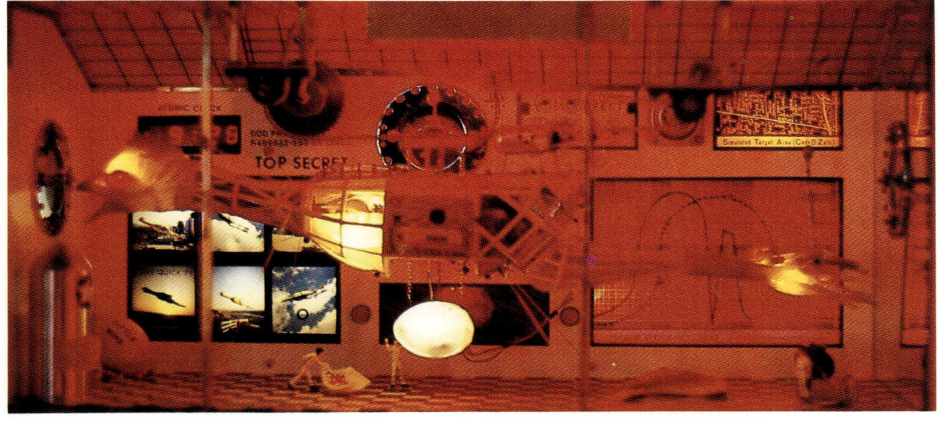

Dave Quick, *Little Nuke,* 1970.
Mixed media. When the viewer pushes a button, the light shifts to red, dials spin, LED's count frantically, and the rubber chicken lays an atomic bomb egg.

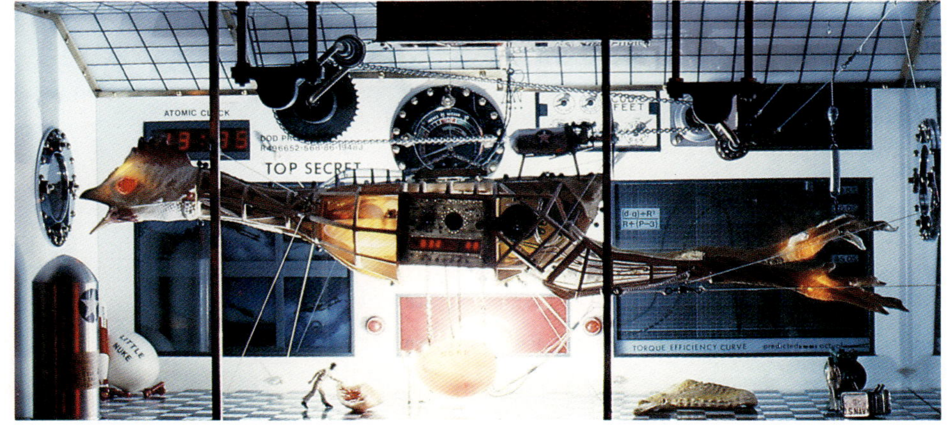

Like most of Quick's works, *Little Nuke* is housed in an aged agricultural crate – the equivalent of blank canvas for an artist who intentionally works in the "found object box art" tradition of American artist Joseph Cornell. Meticulous attention to detail, skilled use of electricity and machine, and intense craftsmanship create intellectual license for Quick's forays into the absurd – he is spoofing technology's own terms.

Hairless Horse Race (1986) is constructed within an old wooden scientific instruments case. The viewer turns a crank which powers not only an electric generator, but two horses that revolve before a cheap plaster reproduction of the *Last Supper.* Christ's head swivels to watch each horse as it goes by, snapping back to watch the next horseman of the Apocalypse. A high-speed flashing strobe light casts huge dancing shadows of the horses on nearby walls. Free from wall current, the work serves as postnuclear holocaust movie projector that can be set up and operated anywhere. The hair has been scraped off not only the horses, but each of the attendees at the *Last Supper,* "so nuclear war survivors won't feel bad about losing their hair," according to the artist.

Mishap at the California Museum of Science and Industry (1984) is an absurd reenactment of a real incident – the Los Angeles museum dropped and broke a one-of-a-kind "lifting body" aircraft donated to it be NASA. A purported cover-up by the museum added great media energy to the unfortunate incident. In Quick's version, the fallen plane is a prostrate rubber chicken and also broken in the accident is "Tom Edison's first light bulb" and the "only intact dinosaur egg ever discovered." The work is spoof of our instant deification of our own technological goods.

In 1984 Quick participated in a group show that ran concurrent with the Los Angeles Olympics – *Homage to Busby Berkeley* was the resultant work. Out of respect to cinema's master of extravaganza, Quick created an extravaganza of his own. Instead of a chorus line of show girls, Quick's extravaganza is sixteen white plastic bulls (four standing, twelve dangling by fish hooks through their noses). Once the viewer pushes a button, for three minutes the bulls bounce, twirl, and spin to the actual movie soundtrack version of "Lullaby of Broadway." The center assembly of the composition is a shelf with four bulls, beneath each is a small plastic hand. In synchronization, the hands rise up through the shelf and scratch the bulls' testicles, while a child's toy spins and emits a "moo" sound. A major wall assembly, *Homage to Busby Berkeley* is arranged into an altar. It is a tongue-in-cheek eighties update of an earlier preholocaust time when Hollywood movies flowed with a fun innocence perhaps forever lost.

PHOTO BY MIKE MAU, COURTESY JOHN MICHAEL KOHLER ARTS CENTER

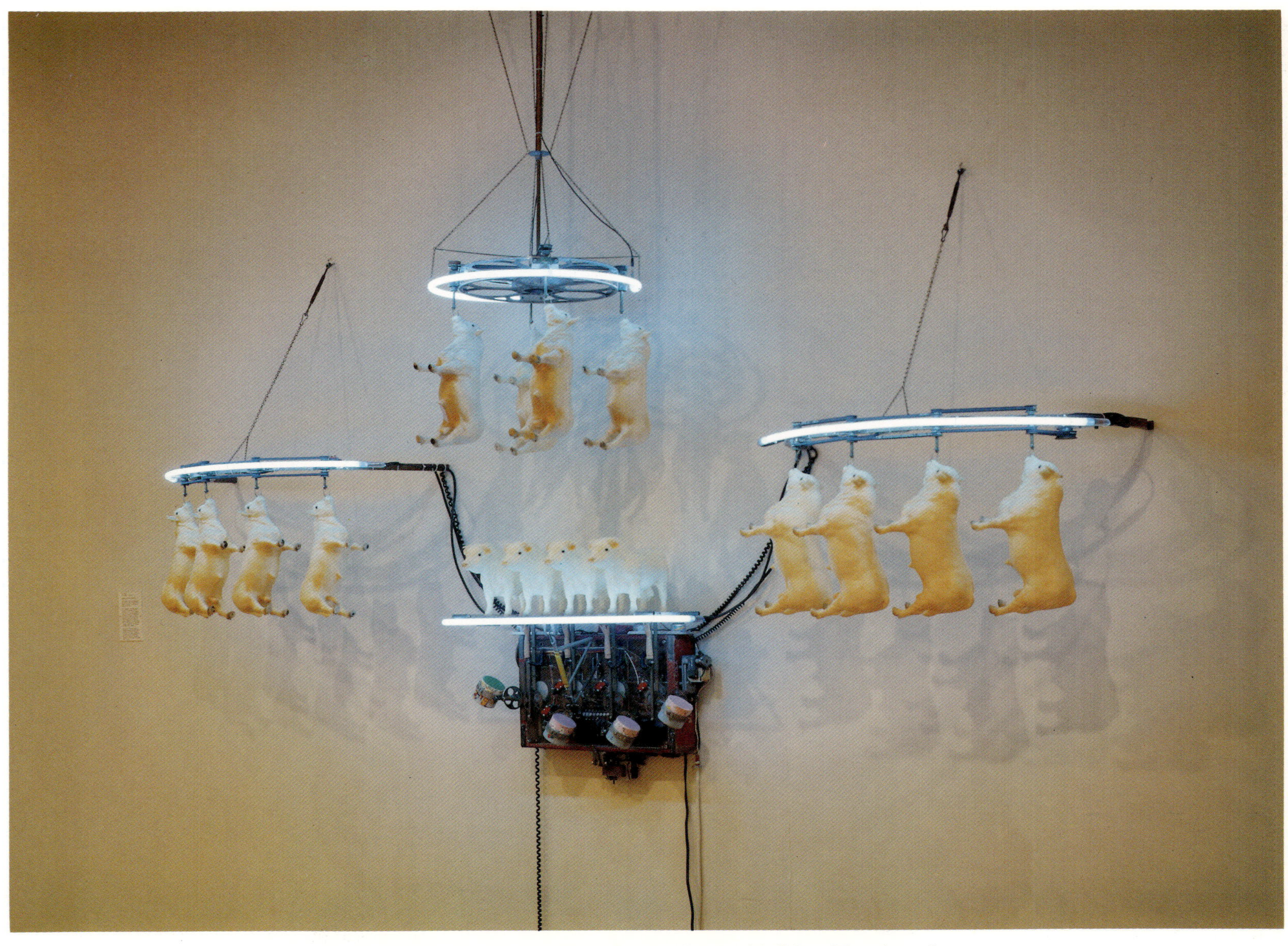

Dave Quick, *Homage to Busby Berkeley,* 1984. Mixed media. While the soundtrack of *Lullaby of Broadway* plays in the background, sixteen white plastic bulls bounce and spin and moo.

Exhumation of Joseph Mengele (1987) is among Quick's most recent works and is his reenactment of the shocking TV footage shot in a Brazilian cemetery the day Mengele's grave was found and disinterred (which footage accompanies the work when shown). The viewer pushes a button and within an old TV set, a zipper is pulled down, and from behind pokes out a plastic human skull. Suddenly, a 1200-watt airline runway bulb turns on with intense heat and light. It snaps off, and the zipper closes – the artist's own rendering of a "rebirth or resurrection of antiChrist."

Quick's work serves as a current event yearbook as it continues to translate topics fresh from the morning headlines and evening news into mechanically pointed sculptural forms. When St. Louis Cardinal second baseman Vince Coleman was run over by a mechanical rain tarp in Busch Stadium, Quick recreated the incident in *Watch Out Vince!* (1986).

Drawing upon the axiom, "judge a society by its least fortunate rather than its most fortunate," Quick uses his menagerie of farm animals and other victims as metaphor for man at the caprice of technology. Man the tool user, or tool the man user? Not unlike the self-directed barnyard revolutionaries in Orwell's *Animal Farm,* Quick elevates the featured characters from his zoo to a plane of power within the context of each piece. The resulting effect is work in which humor and motion lure the viewer into the work, but pointed edges of absurdity, conflict, even despair, eventually surface, just as farm animals eventually surface in the supermarket meat section.

Quick interprets his use of motion as: "It's seductive...a part of the glamour of technology that has won the world and occasionally slaughters whole armies. I use motion to bring viewers close to my work, to confront viewers with a message they otherwise might choose to ignore...and motion is honest to the found objects I use."

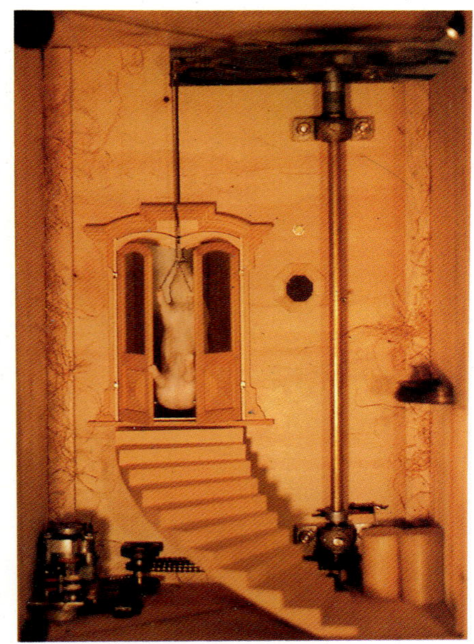

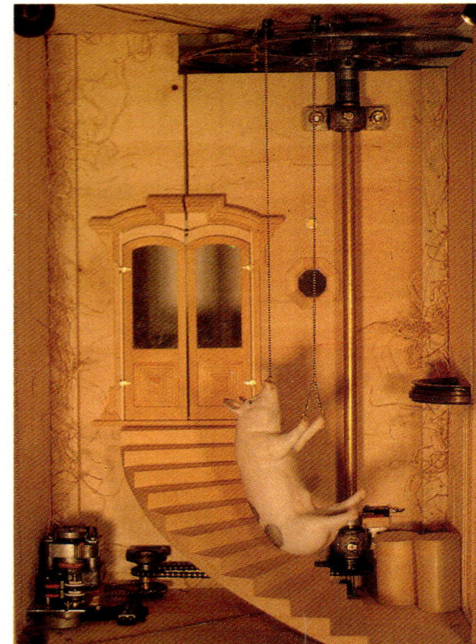

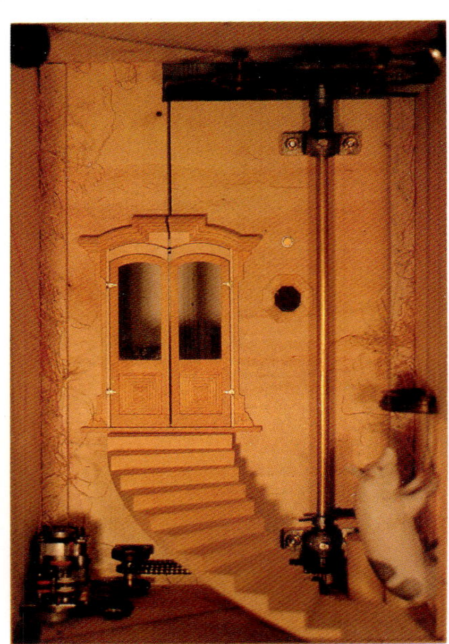

Dave Quick, *Homage to Marcel Duchamp (Pig Descending a Staircase)*, 1984. Mixed media. Upon activation, the empty room's rear doors burst open as a suspended pig enters and appears to slide down the steps, exiting just as quickly through the side doors, out of sight.

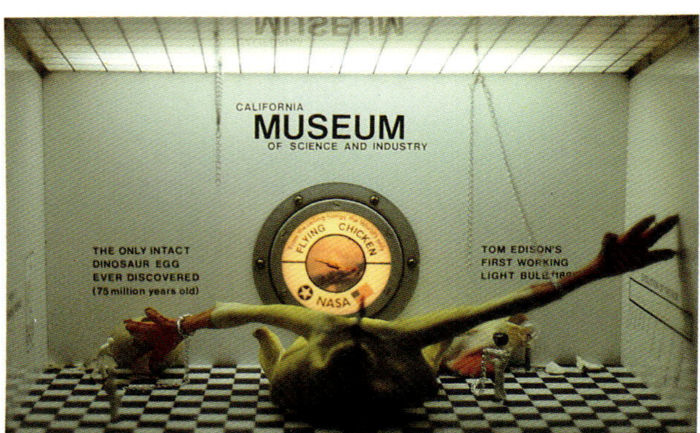

Dave Quick, *Mishap at the California Museum of Science and Industry*, 1984. A rubber chicken crashes to the museum floor, destroying artifacts of our technological world.

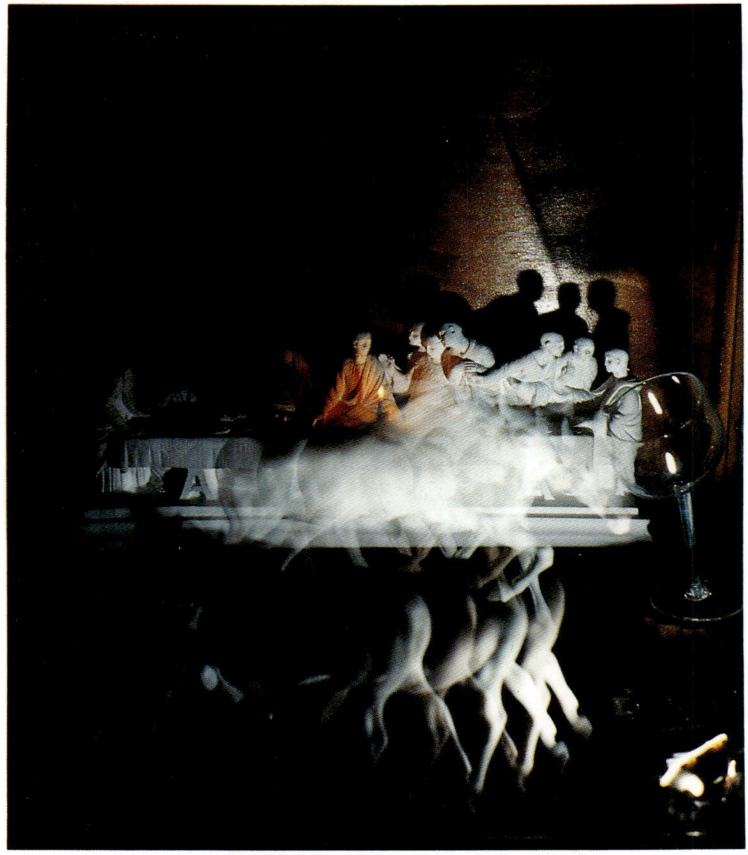

Dave Quick, *Hairless Horse Race*, 1986. Mixed media. A strobe catches horses racing around a plaster reproduction of *The Last Supper*.